U.S. Environmental Protection Agency
Office of Air and Radiation

2007-2008 ACTION PLAN TO INTEGRATE
ENVIRONMENTAL JUSTICE

Table of Contents

Page

OAR Environmental Justice Contacts

Office of Air and Radiation Environmental Justice Coordinator:
Wil Wilson

Office of Air and Radiation Tribal Coordinator:
Darrel Harmon

Office of Air Quality Planning and Standards Contacts:
Gregory Green
Candace Carraway
Lena Epps-Price
Laura McKelvey

Office of Transportation and Air Quality Contacts:
Victor R. McMahan
Kathryn Sargeant
Richard Baldauf
Karen Orehowsky
Jim Blubaugh

Office of Atmospheric Programs Contacts:
Brian McLean
Erika Wilson

Office of Radiation and Indoor Air Contacts:
Elizabeth Cotsworth
Michael Holloway
Anna Duncan

Background: Environmental Justice in the Office of Air and Radiation

The Office of Air and Radiation (OAR) has been actively involved in addressing environmental justice issues since the early 1990's during the advent of the environmental justice movement. In 1992, OAR developed its first Environmental Justice Action Plan which followed the recommendations of the Environmental Equity Work Group in its report to the Administrator entitled, "Environmental Equity: Reducing Risks for All Communities". OAR's efforts to date, have been consistent with the Agency's Environmental Justice Strategy and are characterized by the following four major themes which underscore our environmental justice efforts:

1. **Improve assessment methodology (targeted towards populations suffering disproportional impacts) regarding exposure to air pollution**

    Example Activities: Characterization of populations relative to pollutants; Defining and understanding important determinants of exposure, dose, and effect in different populations that are at high risk from air pollution exposure.

2. **Expanding OAR's outreach, communication and consensus building efforts to low income and minority communities**

    Example Activities: Risk communication model; Cooperative outreach and educational programs; Public informational materials, public service advertising; and information collection activities.

3. **Support and enhance existing and future regional and community-based environmental justice initiatives**

    Example Activities: Cooperative monitoring sites between the U.S. and Mexico to collect pollutant and meteorological data; The study of air toxics through the Mickey Leland Center

4. **Enhance the relationship between OAR and its four adopted institutions in the academic relations program and explore new opportunities to expand this effort**

    Example Activities: Memorandum of Understanding with North Carolina Agricultural and Technical State University which assists in curriculum development, strengthening research capability and promotes the development and training of students/faculty; Memorandum of Understanding with Northern Arizona University to strengthen research, training and public service programs focusing on Native American people and their lands.

Improvements in public health result from OAR programs to (1) reduce emissions of criteria pollutants (i.e., ozone, nitrogen oxides, sulfur dioxide, particulate matter, carbon monoxide, and lead), (2) reduce emissions of air toxics, (3) address issues of climate change, (4) require cleaner vehicles and cleaner fuels, and (5) improve indoor air quality which benefit all citizens (including low income and minority communities and sensitive populations such as those with respiratory illnesses, the elderly, and children).

Since 1970, steps taken under the Clean Air Act have reduced air pollution in the United States by more than 30 percent, producing dramatic health benefits for all Americans. Many of these emission reductions and health benefits have occurred in both urban and rural areas with environmental justice concerns. Everyday, clean air programs across the nation prevent roughly:

- 600 premature deaths;
- 2,000 cases of chronic illness such as asthma and bronchitis;
- 300,000 cases of minor respiratory illness such as aggravated asthma, and;
- 75,000 people from missing work.

Over the past 35 years, the air has become healthier to breathe in more of our cities. Between 1970 and 2005, gross domestic product increased 195 percent, vehicle miles traveled increased 178 percent, energy consumption increased 48 percent, and U.S. population grew by 42 percent. During the same time period, total emissions of the six principal air pollutants dropped by 53 percent.

Since 1991, we have significantly reduced the number of areas not meeting air quality standards. Even though we have made great progress in improving air quality, approximately 122 million people nationwide lived in counties with pollution levels above the National Ambient Air Quality Standards in 2005.

Between 1980 and 2005, average ozone levels decreased 28% as measured using 1-hour data and 20% using 8-hour data. For the same years, ambient concentrations of nitrogen dioxide (NO2) dropped by 37% while sulfur dioxide (SO2) concentrations declined by 63%. Between 1990 and 2005, PM10 levels have gone down by an average of 25%.. PM2.5 levels, which we have been tracking since 1999, decreased 7% from 1999-2005.

In recent years, EPA has acted to dramatically improve America's air quality by providing national programs that when fully implemented will achieve significant reductions in air emissions, such as the NOX Budget Trading Program. During the 2005 ozone season, NOX emissions were 57% lower than in 2000 (before the program was implemented). The Clean Air Interstate Rule (CAIR) adopted in 2005 addresses power plant emissions in 29 eastern states plus the District of Columbia. When fully implemented, CAIR will reduce SO2 emissions in these states by over 70 percent and NOX emissions by over 60 percent from 2003 levels. A closely related action is the EPA Clean Air Mercury rule, the first ever federally-mandated requirements that coal-fired electric utilities reduce their emissions of mercury. Together the Clean Air Mercury Rule and the Clean Air Interstate Rule create a multi-pollutant strategy to reduce emissions throughout the United States. The associated air quality benefits will lead to improved health, longevity and quality of life for all Americans

Clean Air Act requirements for cleaner vehicles/engines and cleaner fuels are one important reason that the nation's air quality is improving. The average new car is over ninety percent cleaner than in 1990. The Tier II program will allow 120 million Americans now living in areas with dangerous pollution levels to enjoy clean air. Other fuel programs already in place provide additional benefits. For example, 30 percent of the gasoline consumed in the U.S., in 18 states, is cleaner-burning reformulated gasoline. Buses, trucks and non-road engines (e.g., bulldozers, locomotives, industrial engines, etc.) also are getting cleaner. Emission standards for locomotives, whose first phase of implementation took effect in 2000-2002, will result in approximately a two-third reduction in NOx emissions (about 650,000 tons per year) and 50 percent reduction in hydrocarbon (HC) and particulate matter emissions. Most of these reductions will be achieved by 2010. In 2002, the Agency promulgated new standards for trucks and buses and diesel fuel, which take effect in 2007. As a result of this program, each new truck and bus will be more than 90 percent cleaner than current models, resulting in a reduction of 2.6 million tons of NOx emissions by 2030. The level of sulfur in highway diesel fuel will be reduced by 97 percent by mid-2006. The Agency recently published regulations to control emissions from a range of unregulated non-road sources, including industrial engines (e.g, forklifts, and generators). The new standards are expected to reduce HC + NOx emissions by approximately 80 percent. In addition, EPA's Clean Air NonRoad Diesel program will reduce emissions from heavy-duty nonroad diesel engines (e.g., agricultural and construction equipment), including new sulfur requirements for non-road diesel fuel.

Toxic emissions are of particular interest to the environmental justice community because of the proximity of many low-income and minority communities to the generators of toxic emissions (e.g., industrial facilities, waste transfer stations, roadways, and bus terminals). EPA rules issued since 1990 are expected to reduce toxic emissions by 2.5 million tons a year from chemical plants, oil refineries, aerospace manufacturing and other industries. As for motor vehicles, programs put in place since 1990 will reduce total air toxics from passenger vehicles in 2030to approximately 80 percent below 1999 levels, as well as reducing pollutants subject to air quality standards. EPA is now working to implement an integrated strategy that is aimed specifically at reducing toxic air pollution in urban areas.

To date, the U.S. and other developed countries have virtually ceased production of CFCs and the other chemicals most damaging to the stratospheric ozone layer, which protects us from ultraviolet radiation that causes skin cancers and cataracts. The Clean Air Act also has achieved significant health benefits by cutting annual SO2 emissions more than 5 million tons from the 1980 level, largely through the market-based acid rain program.

The 1990 Clean Air Act specified in §301(d) that EPA is authorized to treat tribes as 'states' for the purposes of the Act, and that EPA should promulgate regulations specifying how that would be accomplished. In 1995, EPA provided increased funding to tribes in anticipation of the February 1998 promulgation of the Tribal Authority Rule (TAR). In recognition of the unique status of tribes, regulatory authority for Indian country remains the responsibility of the federal government, but under the TAR can be delegated to tribes requesting such authority.

Since 1995, OAR has supported the development of professional and programmatic capacity among tribes to develop and implement air quality management programs to protect resources within the exterior boundaries of the reservation. Tribes have responded with great interest, growing from 7 programs in 1995, to 120 tribes currently receiving grants to develop air programs. In support of those programs, EPA has provided funding to Northern Arizona University to develop a tribal training program that has trained more than a 1000 tribal environmental professionals in various aspects of air quality since 1992. All of OAR's program offices have participated in the rapid growth of the tribal program, providing monitors for all kinds of pollutants from acid rain and mercury to ozone and particulate matter, retrofitting diesel buses, providing training and outreach on indoor air and radiation (there are some housing units in the southwest made from uranium mine waste), and by providing extensive technical support and assistance to tribal nations. OAR initiated efforts to support tribes in Indian country to assess and address risk in areas. We have a pilot effort to conduct Woodstove Changeout and monitor exposure changes on the Nez Perce Nez. We are working with Pleasant Point Passaquatry to conduct fish studies exposure. In addition, OAR proposed a rule to support permitting in Indian country.

Since 1998, OAR staff have worked closely with the National Environmental Justice Advisory Council's (NEJAC) and other grassroots organizations to ensure the integration of environmental justice into our programs, policies, and activities in a manner which is consistent with existing environmental laws and implementing regulations. Our interaction with the NEJAC has proven to be a valuable learning experience. We have learned, for example, that it is important to develop more straightforward approaches to dealing with the community on toxic issues and we have learned that many environmental justice communities have concerns about diesel emissions, bus and truck idling, and emissions trading programs. As a result, we are becoming more able to address the perceptions and concerns of many environmental justice communities. While we are still learning, we are now better equipped to engage in more meaningful dialogue and work with individuals and communities to address environmental justice issues.

Although we have made great strides in improving air quality over the past decade, we realize that additional work must be done to ensure continued public health protection. We are therefore currently pursuing initiatives related to reducing diesel-related emissions, enhancing our diesel retrofit program, reducing mercury emissions, reducing emissions from power plants, reducing air toxics, identifying toxic "hotspots," developing and supporting voluntary programs to reduce emissions, and addressing global climate change. OAR plans to continue our history of developing programs which provide all citizens cleaner air and an opportunity to meaningfully participate in the decision-making processes which may affect their health and well-being.

The Office of Air and Radiation's Environmental Justice Policy

All Americans deserve to be protected from pollution. However, the Office of Air and Radiation recognizes that, in some instances, minority and low income communities face a higher level of environmental risk than the majority population. Therefore, OAR is committed to addressing this issue by incorporating environmental justice into its activities and decision-making processes. The Office's goal is to achieve environmental justice by decreasing the burden of environmental risks to all communities as a result of improved air quality.

OAR staff are expected to consider environmental justice as a meaningful part of our programs and decisions. Thus, as staff decide how to design a new program or to implement existing programs, Our goal is to integrate environmental justice principles into the process. OAR management believes this is the most effective way to ensure that environmental justice is being appropriately addressed.

OAR is also committed to fostering a heightened awareness among our staff working on issues which may effect environmental justice communities. All OAR staff are expected to have a basic knowledge of environmental justice and how they can incorporate the principles of environmental justice into their daily work. Hence, all OAR staff are highly encouraged to participate in the Fundamentals of Environmental Justice workshop developed by the Environmental Justice Training Collaborative---a voluntary, multi-stakeholder, national network initiated in the Fall of 1999 by EPA Regional Offices and the EPA Office of Environmental Justice. OAR actively participated in the development of this workshop and continues to support the work of the Collaborative by assisting in the development of advanced training modules, facilitating training classes, and continuing to provide resources to support this effort.

The Office of Air and Radiation is committed to ensuring good public participation processes. Staff are expected to provide the opportunity for all stakeholder groups which may be affected by our programs to have an opportunity for early and meaningful involvement in the decision-making process. Collaborative efforts to promote the concept of environmental justice are also encouraged. Staff are urged to provide effective outreach to communities which may be affected by our regulations, policies and guidance.

Staff are expected to make every effort to identify areas where minorities and low income populations are being disproportionately exposed to environmental hazards or where there are potential benefits to minority and low income communities (i.e., through transportation and air quality improvements, mass transit policies, and voluntary programs). Once areas of disproportionate impacts are identified, appropriate corrective remedial steps and mitigation procedures should be evaluated.

The Office of Air and Radiation's Environmental Justice Action Plan

The Office of Air and Radiation's Environmental Justice Action Plan is designed to support efforts to develop and implement strategies and activities to integrate environmental justice into existing programs, to further highlight the valuable work we continue to do in the area of environmental justice and to develop a more coordinated environmental justice implementation strategy.

The plan addresses the following areas:

Section 1:Organizational Infrastructure
Section 2:Management Support
Section 3:   Operational Resources
Section 4:Program Support
Section 5:Government Performance and Results Act Alignment
Section 6:   Internal Organizational Engagement
Section 7:   External Stakeholder Engagement
Section 8:   Data Collection, Management, and Evaluation
Section 9:   Professional and Organizational Development
Section 10:   Environmental Justice Assessment
Section 11:   Program Evaluation

Appendix A: Environmental Justice Strategies and Activities Matrix

Section 1: Organizational Infrastructure

- How does your organizational structure promote the integration of environmental justice within all program areas?

The Office of Air and Radiation (OAR) consists of four major program areas: The Office of Air Quality Planning and Standards (OAQPS), the Office of Atmospheric Programs (OAP), the Office of Radiation and Indoor Air (ORIA) and the Office of Transportation and Air Quality (OTAQ). The Office of Policy Analysis and Review (OPAR) is also an integral part of OAR. OPAR consists of policy staff who undertake diverse activities to ensure that OAR policies are consistent, effective in protecting health and the environment, and economically efficient.

OAR has designated a lead Environmental Justice Coordinator in OPAR. Each of OAR's four program offices has also designated environmental justice points of contact (see list in front of this plan) who are responsible for communicating environmental justice-related information to/from the staff in their perspective offices to the lead Environmental Justice Coordinator. This organizational structure promotes the integration and coordination of environmental justice activities within all four of OAR's program areas.

Section 2: Management Support

- How does your Regional/Headquarters office's management communicate expectations about the Environmental Justice Program, review tangible/intangible outcomes, and evaluate performance?

OAR management has clearly communicated to staff that environmental justice considerations will be an integral part of our day-to-day work. OAR has developed Environmental Action Plans since 1992. In the past, OAR has conducted annual monitoring of the environmental justice program to ensure that the Office is achieving our environmental justice goals. However, as part of the implementation of this Action Plan, OAR has developed a mechanism to review progress on a more frequent basis. The goal is for the OAR Environmental Justice Coordinator to hold monthly meetings with the Environmental Justice Contacts from each OAR program office to evaluate progress on the projects described in this Action Plan. Furthermore, the OAR Environmental Justice Contacts will brief the Director of the Office of Policy Analysis and Review Air on a quarterly basis on the progress being made in implementing the Action Plan. The Director of the Office of Policy Analysis and Review is an active member of EPA's Environmental Justice Steering Committee. He provides information from these Steering Committee meetings to staff through the lead Environmental Justice Coordinator. Generally, this type of information is communicated through a series of memorandum to staff.

OAR's management is committed to ensuring that the goal of environmental justice is achieved. To affirm this commitment, OAR sometimes redirects resources from other projects to projects specifically designed to address environmental justice issues. One example is ORIA's Indoor Environments Program. The Indoor Environments Division (IED) annually issues budget guidance emphasizing the importance of environmental justice by strongly encouraging projects that address this issue. This ongoing guidance includes the following:

OPERATING PRINCIPLES
Incorporate the values of environmental justice in our work; make sure we are addressing the needs of those who bear disproportionate risk from indoor air as a result of their socioeconomic status.

UNDERSERVED COMMUNITIES WORKGROUP
This is a new group for 2007 that will consolidate several activities currently housed in Integrated/Multi-Priority and will facilitate plans and services to underserved communities. These projects would be cross-Divisional and would aim to increase the effectiveness and efficiency of the work done by the Teams to meet the needs of groups who are typically hard to reach with our public-health messages.

The Team would be charged with coordinating IED's access to underserved communities, such as Tribes, ethnic minorities, and low-education/low-income families. The group will serve as a central resource to consider strategy and tactics for including such communities in our outreach as a Division. The work group will consider the needs of each community from the recipient's perspective. This will help the Division, to the extent reasonable, approach each community with a cohesive plan or strategy, and not as multiple teams with differing messages on multiple occasions.

IED has identified the following groups to receive initial attention:
- *Tribal/Native American*
- *Head Start*
- *WIC (Women Infant Children)*

Ethnic-specific events (i.e. Congressional black Caucus, Hispanic Heritage Month)

This budget guidance was also distributed to all regional offices.

Section 3: Operational Resources

- Identify the aggregate full-time equivalents (FTE) in your Regional/Headquarters office that specifically focus on environmental justice issues. If responsibilities and duties are parceled out as collateral duties to one or more employees, please compute what the FTE equivalent would be.

- What are the functions and day-to-day responsibilities of your Environmental Justice coordinator(s) and/or team?

Approximately six (6) full-time equivalents (FTEs) in OAR specifically focus on environmental justice issues. Most of these FTEs are performing environmental justice-related work as a collateral duty. The primary responsibility of the OAR environmental justice contacts is to ensure that environmental justice is being considered in all of the work we do and to maximize the use of OAR's statutory authority under the Clean Air Act to address environmental justice issues.

Specifically, OAR's lead Environmental Justice Coordinator:

- Serves as the office's representative during Office of Environmental Justice Monthly Coordinator meetings.

- Develops and manages a multi-disciplinary approach for the Office of Air and Radiation's Environmental Justice Program; provides broad administrative, technical, and program direction and guidance to all environmental justice staff; plans and directs the flow of work for the Environmental Justice Program; assigns priorities and makes work arrangements in response to critical work activities; and develops teams to address the various issues as they are presented.

- In coordination with other programs and offices, develops and implements an Environmental Justice Program which focuses on communication to management and staff of environmental justice issues; communication with internal and external stakeholders; consultation, advocacy, and problem-solving activities; and, coordinating activities with the other environmental justice contacts in OAR to provide the most effective program feasible.

- In conjunction with other offices, develops and implements strategies for achieving the Agency's environmental justice goals.

- Develops and recommends to the senior management, budgets and staffing plans to meet the resource needs of the Environmental Justice Program.

- Represents the headquarters and regional offices in a variety of settings to communicate Environmental Justice Program activities; participates on national environmental justice workgroups; serves as the focal point on coordination of Environmental Justice issues; represents the office in highly visible and controversial discussions with a diverse public; facilitates the maintenance of effective relationships between the Environmental Justice Program and the diverse stakeholders impacted by implementation of OAR regulations and guidance.

Each of the four program offices in OAR has also identified environmental justice contact persons (see list at front of plan). These contacts make up the Environmental Justice Coordinating Council (EJCC) for the Office of Air and Radiation. The mission of the Coordinating Council is to provide cogent and practical recommendations to senior management on how OAR can incorporate environmental justice into day-to-day operations and programmatic responsibilities. The OAR lead Environmental Justice Coordinator will have the responsibility of chairing the EJCC. The responsibilities of the members of the EJCC include, but are not limited to: (1) disseminating information to staff on environmental justice-related issues, (2) ensuring that rules which may affect an environmental justice community are highlighted and that the appropriate staff are assigned to address any issues which may arise, (3) ensuring that citizens have early and meaningful involvement in the decision-making process, (4) promoting the integration of environmental justice, (5) providing consultation and assistance to promote and implement this Action Plan in OAR; and (6) gathering, analyzing, interpreting and providing an environmental justice perspective on relevant information associated with activities conducted by our program office.

Section 4: Program Support

- Does your Regional/Headquarters office have any ongoing mechanisms for focusing on environmental justice issues, such as teams and workgroups? If yes, please list and describe. Also, state how these mechanisms are tied to other programs and activities in your regional/Headquarters office.

- Are there any specific programs/initiatives for which environmental justice are (or should be) listed as a funding priority? If yes, please list or attach.

OAR staff are actively involved in a number of activities designed to make progress in achieving our environmental justice goals. For example, OAR is assisting in (1) the development of better tools to conduct environmental justice analyses, (2) the development of tribal air programs, and (3) the development of environmental justice training. In addition, OAR provides technical and financial support to the National Environmental Justice Advisory Council's Air and Water Subcommittee.

Below is a list of the teams and workgroups serviced by OAR staff which focus on environmental justice-related issues:

OAR Tribal Workgroups: OAR has supported the **National Tribal Air Association (NTAA)**, a tribal air quality organization dedicated to ensuring that tribes set priorities and determine mechanisms for interacting with other governments on air issues. The mission of the NTAA is to collectively advance air quality management policies and programs, consistent with the needs, interests, and unique legal status of American Indian Tribes, Alaska Natives, and Native Hawaiians. The NTAA policies include cooperation with other tribal organizations and workgroups on air-related policies and issues.

In addition, OAQPS has provided support to tribes in applying for CARE grants. And, in conjunction with ORD, OAR is supporting efforts with the Pleasant Point Passamaquoddy Tribe and the Sprit Lake Tribe to conduct risk assessments and develop template guidance for other tribes in conducting risk assessments

Staff from OAR's Office of Radiation and Indoor Air work closely with representatives from the Navajo Nation to develop a strategy for identifying homes with elevated levels of radiation from radioactively contaminated building materials. Some homes may have been built using uranium mill tailings in the mortar, or uranium bearing rocks or building materials from the abandoned mines. When completed, we expect to distribute this strategy for promotion and possible adoption by other tribal nations with similar issues.

Additionally, ORIA works cooperatively with the Institute for Tribal Environmental Professionals (ITEP) at Northern Arizona University. ITEP is developing and implementing outreach and educational efforts to improve community knowledge about radiation science, the hazards of exposure to radiation, and the potential risks associated with abandoned uranium mines.

Office of Environmental Justice Workgroups: A number of OAR staff participate on workgroups formed by the Office of Environmental Justice. These include the **Clean Air Act Permitting Training Module Workgroup, the Environmental Justice Coordinator's Workgroup** and the newly formed **Environmental Justice Coordinating Council.**

OAR also provides funding for a number of specific projects which have environmental justice-related issues (refer to matrix in back of plan for more details):

- **Baltimore Region Environmental Justice and Transportation Project.** EPA's Office of Transportation and Air Quality (OTAQ), the Baltimore Urban League, Baltimore Metropolitan Council, and Morgan State University propose to identify and develop practices and tools to undertake a comprehensive analysis of environmental justice and transportation-related issues in the Baltimore region. The goal of this project is to integrate environmental justice into transportation planning as an on-going and daily activity with meaningful community involvement throughout the process.

- **Hotspot Exposure Assessment Program.** OAR's Office of Transportation and Air Quality, Air Toxics Center has participated in a number of studies that specifically investigated impacts from mobile sources in select microenvironments, including environmental justice communities. These projects included: (1) Fresno Asthmatic Children's Environment Study, (2) Baltimore Traffic Study, and (3) Los Angeles School Bus Exposure Assessment. This and other research has helped quantify impacts from mobile source-generated toxics (for example, in the context of the national mobile source air toxics rule) Ongoing research in other parts of EPA will continue to inform model development and the application of assessment tools (see item immediately below)

- **Predicting Localized Toxics Impacts of Transportation Projects**: OTAQ is developing guidance on how to use models to predict the concentrations of toxic pollutants in the immediate vicinity of proposed transportation projects. This would provide a planning tool for communities and the public when selecting among transportation alternatives and developing mitigation for proposed transportation facilities.

- **Air Toxics Community-based projects:** OAQPS is continuing to assist Regions with the implementation of community-based air toxics programs. The goal is to work with the community, our state and local partner agencies, and other stakeholders to identify solutions to toxic hotspot issues. Since 2000, OAR has provided funds for over 40 community-based projects that are led by the EPA Regional offices. Many of these projects have been used to assess the problems and develop plans for reducing emissions within minority and low-income communities. For example, Oakland, California, is an environmental justice community which is adversely affected by multiple factors, including truck traffic to and from a nearby port, and multiple stationary sources including one major source which produces yeast. Funding was provided to study the communities issues and produce a mitigation strategy. In addition, the State and port have also provided funding for mitigating some of the problems in the area. The community has been actively involved in determining priorities for these initiatives.

- **Community Action for a Renewed Environment (CARE):** CARE is a new initiative, founded in OAR, involving cross-Agency collaborative partnerships. In December 2006, the Office of Air and Radiation transferred Agency management lead for the CARE program to the Office of Pollution Prevention and Toxics Substances. OAR Immediate Office staff members, Larry Weinstock and Marva King, continue to lead CARE activities on the cross-Agency headquarters administrative team. Through CARE's community-based, community-driven, multiple environmental pollutant cooperative agreement program to reduce toxics, EPA works with state, local and tribal government agencies and various local organizations, including non-profits, citizens, businesses, and schools helping create collaborative partnerships to address toxics in their local environment. CARE empowers communities to improve their environment through local action, providing technical support and federal funding directly to these collaborative partnerships working at the local level.

  Through CARE, EPA solicits proposals for two different types of competitive grants to tribal and local governments, community organizations, and NGOs. The smaller grants support the development of community based stakeholder groups to assess local toxics risks. The larger grants are for communities that have already organized and assessed risks and are ready to select risk reduction activities. From 2005-2006, the CARE program awarded twenty-nine community projects and held two annual national training workshops. In 2007, the program anticipates awarding between ten to fifteen community projects and holding its third annual national training workshop. Twenty-seven of the twenty-nine CARE projects are located in economically distressed project areas.

- **Guidance to Reduce Toxics in Local Communities.** EPA has also produced a draft guidance which describes a method that State, Tribal and Local governments can use to work with their communities in developing a plan that lays out multimedia sources of pollution (air, water and hazardous waste), specific activities and goals for reducing pollution and a framework for strong public participation. OAR and OSWER are currently funding a pilot project in Phoenix, Arizona to demonstrate the use of the guidance. Region 9, Arizona Department of Environmental Quality and multiple local organizations have developed a stakeholder group of all interested parties to discuss their issues and how to best address them. In addition, the State and EPA have conducted inspections at facilities of concern in the community and are working on pollution prevention options for several industries.

- **National Clean Diesel Campaign.** OAR will continue to support diesel retrofit programs as a cost-effective solution for lowering emissions from diesel exhaust in communities across the nation. This Program is a non-regulatory, incentive based, innovative program designed to pursue reductions in hydrocarbons, nitrogen oxides, carbon monoxide, and particulate matter from existing diesel vehicles and equipment by the installation of pollution-reducing technology.

  As part of this program, OAR and the regions have established diesel retrofit projects in hundreds of communities nationwide. In addition, EPA's Clean School Bus USA program, started in 2003, has addressed school bus fleets across the nation, including many located in areas of disproportional environmental impacts. These programs promote the use of advanced emission control equipment reducing pollution from existing fleets.

  Congress has provided approximately $30 million for clean diesel projects from FY 2003 through FY 2006. In addition, it is expected that FY 2007 funds (approximately $12 million) will result in similar clean diesel projects; the vast majority will benefit children and other sensitive populations.

  A menu of tribal options for grants is also being developed to stimulate proposals from tribal organizations for funding projects.

  Competitive proposals for funding which address environmental justice issues in the areas served by the projects are required. Thirty-five Clean School Bus (CSB) grants and 10 NCDC projects were awarded with FY 2005 funds. All (100%) of the CSB projects targeted children. Thirty (86%) of those CSB projects involved areas with higher than average poverty levels for children less than 18 and/or were in areas in non-attainment for PM and/or Ozone. 17 (49%) of the CSB projects are in areas with higher than average poverty levels for children. Nine (9) of the 10 (90%) NCDC projects targeted areas in ozone and/or PM non-attainment areas or had a higher than the national average poverty rate for children less than 18 years old. 70% of the NCDC projects were in areas with either PM or Ozone non-attainment concerns. For FY 2008 and beyond, as provisions in the Energy Policy Act of 2005 are implemented, priorities for clean diesel projects will include alleviating disproportional environmental impacts on sensitive populations.

- **Clean School Bus USA**. In April 2003, EPA launched "Clean School Bus USA," a children's health program aimed at reducing air pollution from school buses. This program is part of EPA's National Clean Diesel Campaign.

  Across the country, 25million children ride school buses spending between 20 minutes and several hours per day on these vehicles. Unfortunately, older school buses can pollute up to sixty times more than the newest buses using clean technology. Children are especially vulnerable to the effects of diesel emissions which can cause respiratory disease and exacerbate long term conditions such as asthma. Reducing pollution from school buses will help improve local air quality and reduce children's exposure to diesel exhaust. Children in environmental justice areas who suffer from asthma caused by diesel exhaust will benefit by the removal of one more asthma trigger.

Clean School Bus USA has three primary goals:

- Reduce unnecessary school bus idling 100% by 2010.
- Retrofit and upgrade 100% of the existing 1990-2003 diesel school buses by 2010.
- Replace 100% of pre-1990 school buses with new clean buses.

To financially support this effort, Congress provided almost $25 million from FY 2003-FY 2006 for a cost-shared grant program designed to assist school districts in upgrading their bus fleets. Congress also included $7 million in EPA's FY 2007 budget for clean school bus projects. In solicitations for Clean School Bus USA projects, disproportional environmental impacts on the local population is listed as one of the factors that EPA considers in evaluating proposals. OAR strongly indicated that one of our goals is to improve the health of communities that are considered low-income, have high asthma rates, and/or receive a disproportionate amount of pollution from diesel vehicles.

OAR is also working directly with tribes to reduce children's exposure to diesel exhaust from their commute to school on buses. For example, OAR awarded a grant to the Puyallup tribe in the state of Washington to establish a clean diesel retrofit project. This project involved installing advanced emission control technologies on their school bus fleet that will reduce particulate levels of the bus's exhaust by over 90 percent. An objective of this project was to address the disproportionate exposure risk for minority children that live in this tribal community.

- **SmartWay Transport Partnership**. The movement of goods or freight involves the use of large diesel engines and areas with high concentrations of diesel truck and engine activity can have significant concentrations of air pollutants. The goal of EPA's SmartWay Transport Partnership is to create incentives for the transportation industry to adopt cleaner and more fuel efficient vehicles. We accomplish this goal through a variety of methods. For example, we:

  - Recruit shipping companies (e.g., Ikea) to commit to ship 50% or more of their goods on SmartWay qualifying trucking companies
  - Recruit trucking companies to adopt technologies and strategies that will achieve greater fuel economy and reduce emissions
  - Award grants to evaluate and deploy technologies and strategies that assist partners with achieving their goals
  - Provide public recognition and brand/logo recognition for cleaner and more efficient transportation
  - Educate the public and transportation industry about methods to save money and improve air quality

  When it comes to identifying and improving air quality in areas with potential environmental justice-related concerns, the SmartWay program has two strategies. First, we issue grant awards to evaluate and deploy technologies that will reduce emissions and conserve fuel. Our solicitations for proposals typically include a ranking or general consideration of environmental and compliance-related factors to assist in making fair and efficient decisions. Based on the proposals received, we apply all ranking factors and considerations in our selection of grant recipients. In many cases, we have awarded projects in communities with potential environmental justice related concerns .[1] However, grant awards are subject to EPA appropriations and may not occur every year.

  The second strategy, and mainstay of the program, is deploying "SmartWay Upgrade Kits" on trucks and promoting the "SmartWay Truck." The SmartWay Upgrade Kit and Truck involve converting a truck into a cleaner and more energy efficient vehicle. The upgrade kit consists of an idle reduction device (e.g., auxiliary power unit), wide-based tires, tractor-trailer aerodynamics, and an emissions control device. Combined, these components will achieve up to a 19% reduction in oxides of nitrogen and a 50-80% reduction in particulate matter. The SmartWay Truck is similar, in that, we have created a certification for a truck that meets specific fuel saving and emission reduction criteria.

---

[1] In FY 05 and '06, EPA awarded several grants that benefit EJ areas. For example, EPA awarded $60K to a project (total project cost with partner support - $200K) to evaluate idle reduction equipment on 7 locomotive engines in a low-income, minority neighborhood in Chicago.

To deploy the SmartWay Upgrade Kit or Truck, we create financial opportunities for truck owners to purchase these technologies. For example, working with the Small Business Administration, US Department of Agriculture, and others, we have created various loan packages for truck owners. The loan packages all provide lower cost loans. The USDA program involves working with community development banks to assist trucking companies located in rural areas, defined as having a population less than 25,000 which may also include low income or minority areas.

SmartWay selects pilot projects that bring together certain key components.

- Availability of lower cost loans through community development banks, as determined by the banks ability and willingness to participate in the SmartWay program.
- Presence of truck dealerships and service centers capable and willing to install SmartWay Upgrade Kits
- Counties designated by EPA as nonattainment or maintenance for ozone and/or particulate matter, and
- Other relevant environmental and compliance related factors including an analysis of relevant potential EJ-related concerns and demographic information.

Taking the four components identified above, SmartWay will be better able to enact a uniform, fair and efficient plan to recruit truck owners who reside in areas with: (1) readily available funding mechanisms, (2) nonattainment/maintenance designation and other relevant environmental and compliance factors, (3) proximity to truck dealerships and service centers, and (4) a consideration of potential environmental justice-related concerns.

SmartWay is also developing a program to reduce diesel emissions from drayage and regional trucking operations. These trucks are frequently older, travel through areas with potential EJ-related concerns and emit higher levels of emissions. Again, SmartWay is working in public and private partnerships to develop low cost financing options to help small and medium sized trucking companies purchase trucks equipped with after-treatment exhaust devices. OTAQ expects to use some of the funds authorized by Congress as part of the Diesel Emission Reduction (DERA) program to help leverage some of these options. SmartWay is also developing an assessment tool that can be used by marine and rail terminals to estimate local drayage emissions. This tool will allow for the evaluation of different operational strategies, like improved gate operations and chassis pools, that can help reduce truck idling and total vehicle miles driven.

EPA's SmartWay Transport Program includes an initiative to reduce air pollution and Conserve fuel from idling trucks and locomotives. As part of this program, OTAQ is organizing a regional coalition of communities, state and local governments, and trucking and truck stop companies to install idle reduction systems along major interstate corridors, (such as I-65 in the Midwest and I-95 in the Northeast). The criteria for identifying locations include areas with low-income, minority populations in proximity to a disproportionate number of facilities. Two such locations include a large truck stop in Gary, Indiana which received a $125,000 grant for the installation of truck stop electrification infrastructure, and a locomotive switch yard which received a $60,000 grant for anti-idling devices.

- **Major and Minor New Source Review (a.k.a Tribal NSR rule).** On August 21, 2006, OAR proposed the Tribal NSR rule to address significant regulatory gaps in the protection of air quality in Indian country. The Tribal NSR rule will address new and modifying stationary major and minor air pollution sources. Currently, minor sources in Indian country are unregulated. In addition, we do not currently have a permitting mechanism for major sources in non-attainment areas in Indian country. Tribes have expressed concerns about the potential for cumulative impacts and un-level playing fields for economic development. This a pilot project for tribal consultation. OAR hopes to develop this new rule with sensitivity to the needs and culture of tribes and with attention to the impact of our actions on tribal sovereignty. After proposal, we held a number of outreach activities on the content of the proposal including web training and face-to-face meetings in Chicago, Phoenix, Temecula CA, and Seattle. We expect to complete the rulemaking this fall.

- **Asthma Initiative.** Since indoor environmental pollutants are important asthma triggers, it is the goal of OAR's indoor environmental asthma initiative to integrate indoor environmental management into medical and health care asthma management practices. This initiative is targeted to reach nearly 7 million children living with asthma, particularly those in low income families that are disproportionately affected by the disease. The initiative establishes a national public education and prevention program in response to the asthma epidemic in the United States. The goal of the education and prevention program is to raise public awareness of indoor environmental asthma triggers (e.g., secondhand smoke, dust mites, mold, pet dander, and cockroaches) and recommend actions that can be taken to reduce children's exposure to the triggers in homes, schools and child care settings. OAR is working to insure that environmental management is fully incorporated into all asthma education and disease management programs.

- In New Haven, CT, OAR funded the Community Clean Air Initiative, which is co-managed by the New Haven Health Department and the City Plan Department. The project developed and implemented a risk reduction strategy for prioritized air toxics sources. The local inventory provided credibility and a firm basis for the workgroup to focus on areas of concern in a 3-prong approach: transportation, industrial sources such as surface coaters, and degreasers, and fossil fuel reduction and indoor air sources. Specific projects include the purchase of ultra low sulfur diesel fuel for the entire municipal fleet of about 120 school buses, garbage trucks, maintenance equipment and fire trucks; pollution prevention workshops for surface coaters and degreasers; a Smoke Outside asthma reduction initiative that focused on school and public health nurses, health and day care centers

- OAR funded a monitoring study and risk assessment which found unacceptable screening levels of air toxics in Jefferson County, Kentucky, which relied on collaboration among the community (including industry), local and state air agencies, University of Louisville, and EPA. This led to negotiations between the greatest sources of some of the most serious pollutants and the local government (mayor's office and air program) to reduce those emissions. It has also supported the development of risk based air toxics regulations for Jefferson County, Kentucky.

- The St. Louis Community Air Project is a broad-based collaborative effort that has focused on 1) indoor air toxics 2)diesel emission reductions 3) improved emissions inventory and pollution prevention assistance for small businesses and 4) efforts to focus on "greener buildings" by working with the St. Louis Chapter of the U.S. Green Building Council. Early successes included retrofitting diesel school buses, an idling reduction initiative, and community capacity building on air toxics reduction practices.

- The Great American Woodstove Change-out is primarily a voluntary partnership approach that addresses the challenge of motivating homeowners and communities to replace their old, polluting woodstoves with new, safer, more efficient and cleaner burning technology (e.g., EPA-certified woodstove) and to educate them to burn more cleanly. The project furthers both of the Agency's National Environmental Justice Priorities by reducing the number of asthma attacks caused by exposure to particulate matter and reducing exposure to air toxics.

- Along with EPA Region 8, OAR partnered with, Lincoln County, MT, Hearth Patio and Barbecue Association (HPBA), and the State of Montana to begin replacing up to 1200 woodstoves with cleaner burning hearth appliances in the Libby, Montana area. As part of the larger EPA-led Great American Woodstove Change-out campaign, this partnership has worked to garner resources and to educate the public about clean wood burning techniques and about the importance of proper woodstove and chimney maintenance. The Libby, Montana woodstove change-out campaign was kicked off in June of 2005. We expect that by the end of the 2007, there will be 950 change-outs. The partners developed replacement criteria and a program schedule, and the industry jumpstarted the program by contributing $1 million in woodstoves, chimneys and installation – enough to replace old stoves for about 300 low-income Libby families. Other resources were leveraged from EPA, the state of Montana and Congress. Monitors for both PM2.5 and air toxics were purchased and installed along existing monitors. Additional outcomes include: improved indoor air quality as new stoves will be properly vented and sealed, a 50% improvement in energy efficiency, use of 1/3 less wood, and a reduction of the risk of chimney fires due to a cleaner burn and less creosote build-up. Water quality will likely improve because of lower pollutant deposition (benzo(a)pyrene) into nearby waters, including the Kalispell River.

Section 5: Government Performance and Results Act (GPRA) Alignment (link to mission and priorities):

• How is your Regional/Headquarters office's environmental justice program linked to your Regional/Headquarters office's main GPRA priorities?

• How are your Regional/Headquarters office's environmental justice strategies and activities integrated into specific programmatic areas/functions? (e.g., permitting, community outreach, etc.)

• Does your Regional/Headquarters office utilize Performance Partnership Agreements (PPAs) and Performance Partnership Grants (PPGs) to specifically address environmental justice issues? If yes, please list and describe.

The Office of Air and Radiation does not have GPRA goals which separately address environmental justice. OAR's current GPRA goals focus on protecting human health and the environment through implementation of our criteria pollutant and toxics programs. Consistent with the information provided in this plan, OAR's goal is to provide clean air for everyone, regardless of their race or socioeconomic background. Therefore, environmental justice considerations are an integral part of all of OAR's GPRA goals. The following three examples illustrates OAR's efforts to integrate environmental strategies into our ongoing programmatic activities.

Under one of OAR's current GPRA goals, ORIA is responsible for overseeing the safe disposal in the Waste Isolation Pilot Plant (WIPP) of radioactive waste from approximately 20 sites around the country. The Department of Energy (DOE) manages waste disposal operations related to the WIPP. The removal of waste from surface storage, and its isolation in a single, underground location, will facilitate the cleanup and closure of DOE sites contaminated with radioactive materials. ORIA is sensitive to the interests and concerns of communities affected by WIPP, and has taken action to solicit input from communities and minority groups. This public comment/response program will help address many of the environmental justice-related concerns associated with the placement and operation of DOE sites.

ORIA's Las Vegas laboratory facility provides direct support toward increasing the number of indoor radon gas measurements in the homes of economically-disadvantaged residents. ORIA's laboratory provides a large supply of no-cost home radon test kits to individuals and/or organizations that work with targeted populations in local communities. Under this program, ORIA assists with the laboratory analysis of the home radon tests, sends final test results, and maintains a database on the number and location of kits that were analyzed during each fiscal year.

To better assist tribes, OAR is working to provide technical assistance and program support to build tribal capacity in addressing indoor and outdoor air concerns. OAR is working to develop federally based programs which would enable EPA to address Indian Country air quality problems where tribes may be unable to do so themselves.

Section 6: Internal Organizational Engagement

- Does your Regional/Headquarters office's environmental justice program have any ongoing mechanisms to communicate with, receive input from, and otherwise consistently engage with other programs in your Regional/Headquarters office? If yes, please list and describe.
- Has your Regional/Headquarters office developed any related guidance to the staff regarding the integration of environmental justice in areas such as authorization/delegation, environmental education, grants and contracts, inspection, enforcement and compliance assistance, permitting, performance partnership, public participation, waste site cleanup/brownfields, etc.? If yes, please list and describe.

Staff from the Office of Air and Radiation engage in frequent meetings with staff from the Office of Environmental Justice to ensure that OAR's environmental justice program is consistent with Agency policy and direction. Because the Agency is moving toward a multi-media approach to addressing environmental issues, OAR consistently collaborates with other media offices to ensure that our program goals are consistent when issues related to air pollution are raised. Specific issues/projects may require more frequent communications with other programs. Listed below are a number of collaborative efforts in which OAR staff are involved:

- EPA's Children's Health Initiative
- Agency Asthma Initiatives;
- Community for a Renewed Environment (CARE) program
  Policies on mercury emissions;
- Policies related to the deposition of air pollutant into water bodies. Because of the unique relationship between air deposition and water pollution issues, OAR collaborates on a regular basis with the Office of Water on environmental justice related issues through the NEJAC Air and Water Subcommittee;
- The National Environmental Justice Training Collaborative. Through the work of the collaborative, OAR is kept up-to-date on the latest environmental justice training initiatives;
- Regularly scheduled meetings with other Headquarters and Regional EJ Coordinators;
- Involvement with the EPA Environmental Justice Steering Committee
- Policies on near-roadway exposure assessment (this includes work with the Office of Federal Activities on NEPA Policy as well as coordination with the North American Commission for Environmental Cooperation).

OAR proactively pursues opportunities to integrate environmental justice into our program. This expectation has been consistently communicated to staff through our action plans and memorandums.

Section 7: External Stakeholder Engagement

- Does your Regional/Headquarters office have any processes in place to receive input on environmental justice issues from external stakeholders, such as workgroups, advisory bodies, or listening sessions? If yes, please describe the process and explain how the input gathered may be (or has been) used by your Regional/Headquarters office.
- Does your Regional/Headquarters office have any ongoing mechanisms to share information to external groups regarding environmental justice such as websites, faxback system, printed outreach materials, etc.? If yes, please list and describe. Also please mention the specific stakeholder group(s) which benefit from these outreach mechanisms.
- How does your Regional/Headquarters office identify stakeholders who could benefit from increased awareness about environmental justice and being more engaged in the collaborative problem-solving process?
- How does your Regional/Headquarters office promote collaborative problem-solving among stakeholders?
- Does your Regional/Headquarters office have any special initiatives or provisions to address issues for persons with limited English proficiency? If yes, please describe or attach.
- In the course of your environmental justice outreach, does your Regional/Headquarters office utilize any informational materials translated in languages other than English? If yes, please list and describe.
- Are there any specific grant programs for which environmental justice was listed as funding priority? Please list and describe.

The Clean Air Act requires that the public have the opportunity to participate in the regulatory process. Therefore, OAR staff meets frequently with external stakeholders who may be affected by or who may have a vested interest in the rules and guidance the Office develops. With respect to environmental justice groups, OAR works closely with Office of Environmental Justice staff to identify such stakeholders. This interaction with external stakeholders may take many forms including, but, not limited to the following: (1) a meeting with industry or an environmental group, (2) a public hearing or public listening session, (3) through the public comment period required for all rulemakings, or (4) through workgroups formed under the Federal Advisory Council Act (FACA). OAR also engages in dialogue with groups such as the Northeast States for Coordinated Air Use Management and the National Association of Clean Air Agencies, to get a better understanding of how states and local air quality control agencies may be affected by the actions of our office.

OAR works closely with two Federal Advisory Groups, the National Environmental Justice Advisory Council (NEJAC) and the Clean Air Act Advisory Committee (CAAAC). Staff is always present at NEJAC meetings and provides support as needed. When appropriate, OAR also brings environmental justice related issues to the attention of the Clean Air Act Advisory Committee (CAAAC). The Office of Air and Radiation is sensitive to the public health and environmental concerns of affected tribal and other communities through its radiation activities.

For example, two of ORIA's regulatory programs are the Waste Isolation Pilot Plant (WIPP) and Yucca Mountain. Both of these facilities are designed, owned, and operated by the Department of Energy. ORIA develops the public health and safety standards for WIPP, conducts audits and inspections, and serves as the regulator for WIPP. Public health and safety standards were also developed for Yucca Mountain. ORIA's laboratories have performed public consultation and developed a communications needs assessment to understand 1) what the public's concerns were about the WIPP project, 2) what their informational needs were, and 3) how best to communicate with them. Notices advertising the public hearings were placed in English and Spanish newspapers. Additionally, the services of a Spanish translator were provided at WIPP public hearings. During the development of our Yucca Mountain standards, ORIA met with state and local representatives and representatives from many Native American tribes to explain roles and regulations and listen to public concerns.

Currently, the Office of Transportation and Air Quality (OTAQ) and the NEJAC are undertaking a collaborative effort to examine the impacts to communities from the transportation of freight - also known as goods movement. Freight transportation, the movement of goods using trucking, rail and ships, is an integral part of the U.S. economy. However, freight movement involves the use of large diesel engines which are a major source of air pollutants including oxides of nitrogen (NOx), particulate matter (PM), greenhouse gas emissions, and fuel use. OTAQ employs several innovative public private efforts to address freight issues including the SmartWay Transport Partnership (SWT) and National Clean Diesel Campaign (NCDC). OTAQ's goal is to achieve reductions of up to 19% in NOx 50-80% in PM, and by 2012, reduce CO_2 emissions by 33-66 million metric tons and save 150 million barrels of oil (equal to 12 million cars off the road). Since an initial meeting in September 2007, OTAQ and the NEJAC are forming a working group with representatives from various interests including business, science, and community to examine how to further facilitate current and indentify innovative ways to address the complex issues involved in the movement of goods. For example, SmartWay Transport is working closely with the NEJAC to identify and expand financial and market-based incentives that challenge the freight industry to improve its environmental performance while reducing operating cost and providing greater energy security. SmartWay Transport's goal is to develop sustainable financing strategies to provide truck companies and owner-operators access to financing options to help pay for technologies that not only reduce fuel use and air pollution but also subsequent impacts to communities. Upgraded trucks financed with SmartWay's low interest program are less expensive and more environmentally efficient than the same truck not upgraded and many of these trucks are drayage and regional trucks which are frequently older, emit more air pollutants, and often driven by low-income and minority drivers.

ORIA's Indoor Environments Division has developed and implemented a nationwide grants competition which is focused on one-on-one public education regarding asthma and other indoor air issues in low income communities. The competition guidance required applicants to include environmental justice in their proposals. The most recent guidance stated:

EPA strives to improve indoor air quality (IAQ) and reduce associated human health risks (such as asthma attacks) posed by pollutants in indoor environments/building *types. This is accomplished by increasing awareness and understanding of indoor air quality principles and risks as well as by promoting appropriate voluntary practices and risk reduction actions to improve indoor air quality by the public and key stakeholders. EPA is also committed to working <u>with disproportionately impacted populations and tribes</u> to reduce risks from poor IAQ.*

ORIA's Indoor Environments Division (IED) has recognized the need to reach diverse audiences in order to effectively reduce health risks and uses a wide variety of approaches and techniques including the following:

- All major publications are translated bilingually, including Spanish and other major languages.

- The IED home page contains a "Recursos en Espanol" button that can be "clicked," and directs the user to all available Spanish publications.

- The national radon and asthma media campaigns are developed and aired in both Spanish and English

- The development of a low literacy brochure on asthma for national distribution.

In addition to the activities listed above, ORIA's works with a wide variety of other public national organizations that have extensive regional and local networks and share mutual goals with the program such as the protection of public health and establishment of local efforts to stimulate public action through media and grassroots efforts. ORIA supports national organizations with extensive regional and local networks to help establish local environmental justice outreach programs. This support is accomplished by establishing and encouraging partnerships with organizations that have the unique ability to reach special populations. OAR meets regularly with these groups in order to create new opportunities for achieving significant risk reduction. Funding is provided to cooperative partners in support of developing new tools for building community based programs that are flexible enough to be responsive to the needs of residents in local communities. Some examples of funded activities include the following:

- National Safety Council – work with Hispanic promoters on asthma.
- Association of Clinicians for the Underserved-asthma education to low income families
- Intertribal Council of Arizona – "Circuit rider" to do asthma education
- National Association Inter-Tribal Council of Michigan-Educate Native American
       Mothers and Caregivers to reduce second hand smoke exposure to children
- American Lung Association – developed and distributed a publication entitled *Building Successful Indoor Air Quality and Environmental Justice Programs.*
- Wake Forest University-Train health educators to work with Hispanic migrant workers and educate Head Start families

– American Medical Association-Train physicians who serve low-income, low-education families

Thousands of schools have implemented indoor air management plans as a result of OAR's Indoor Air Quality Tools for Schools program resulting in thousands of students and staff working and attending school classrooms each day with improved indoor air quality. Furthermore, OAR staff have worked with other organizations and developed and piloted courses for school officials and facility managers which help explain the benefits of Performance Contracting in improving building conditions and reducing energy use by improving indoor air quality.

As a result of the work of OAR's radon risk reduction program – 20% of all schools have been tested, about 632 thousand homes have an operating mitigation system and about 1.42 million homes have been built with radon-resistant features.

OAR continues to support tribal programs in many ways by including tribal representatives on policy groups like the CAAC and the National Monitoring Strategy Workgroup, ensuring that they are involved in ongoing Regional Planning Organizations to address regional haze and other issues. Notably, where tribes choose not to participate, OAR takes seriously its obligation to implement federal programs on reservations where it is necessary and appropriate to protect human health and the environment.

OAR has recognized the need to both educate and inform the public on the work we are doing to improve public health and the environment. To this end, OAR has developed outreach materials geared toward informing communities of many of the programs that are underway. A number of our informational brochures have also been translated to Spanish. Copies of most of these materials can be found through the EPA website at www.epa.gov. Below is a list of some of the environmental justice-related outreach resources which are available:

- **National Radon Hotline [1-800-SOS-RADON (1-800-767-7236)].**
  The Office of Radiation and Indoor Air is providing a grant to the National Safety Council to reach culturally-diverse populations through the staffing and operation of the bilingual Hotline which responds to public requests for IAQ information and referrals. The hotline supports increasing radon testing and mitigation in Hispanic communities through follow-up with consumers requesting the radon test kit coupons, and providing information about many other indoor air quality health issues (e.g. mercury, secondhand smoke exposure to children, etc.).

- **Indoor Air Quality Tools for Schools Website (http://www.epa.gov/iaq/schools/)**
  The Indoor Air Quality Tools for Schools website is designed to strengthen and expand EPA's national outreach program that is designed to create healthier indoor environments for children in our nations schools by providing tools and resources to spur the use of the Indoor Air Quality Tools for Schools Kit.

- **Waste Isolation Pilot Plant (WIPP) National Information Hotline.** Based on feedback from stakeholders ORIA has addressed the communications needs of culturally-diverse communities by developing a toll-free (1-800) information line. The general public can access the line 24 hours per day and 7 days per week to hear recorded messages about current and planned EPA activities and opportunities for public involvement. Because New Mexico and other affected states have a large Hispanic population, the WIPP Information Line message is available in both English and Spanish. Many of our public information brochures and materials are also available in both English and Spanish.

- **Waste Isolation Pilot Plant (WIPP) National Website (www.epa.gov/radiation/wipp) and (www.epa.gov/radiation/yucca).** The ORIA website provides the general public with access to important information about WIPP and Yucca Mountain.

- **Asthma Website (http://www.epa.gov/iaq/asthma/).** ORIA's Indoor Environments Division has launched a national public and prevention program in response to the asthma epidemic in the United States. The website is designed to raise public awareness of indoor environmental asthma triggers and actions that can be taken to reduce children's exposure in homes, schools and child care settings. The website provides public information about tools and resources, primary contacts, asthma triggers, and answers to other frequently asked questions.

- **TribalAIR Website (http://www.epa.gov/oar/tribal/airprogs.html).** The TribalAIR web site is designed to strengthen EPA and Tribal air quality programs in Indian Country by: providing timely and user-friendly access to key information; promoting the exchange of ideas; and making available relevant documents to all environmental professionals who live and work in Indian Country.

- **The TribalAir Newsletter** is a quarterly newsletter produced by OAR's Office of Air Quality Planning and Standards as one of our tools to make Tribal air professionals aware of our air pollution control activities early enough allow tribes to participate in their development. This newsletter provides information on upcoming activities (e.g., workshops and training) as well as, a place to report progress.

- **Air Quality Index Booklet and Air NOW Website** (http://www.epa.gov/airnow). OAR is working to make information about air quality as available to the public as information about the weather. A key tool in this effort is the Air Quality Index (AQI). EPA and local officials use the AQI to provide the public with timely and easy-to-understand information on local air quality and whether air pollution levels pose a health concern. The AQI booklet tells you about the AQI and how it is used to provide air quality information. It also tells you about the possible health effects of major air pollutants at various levels and suggests actions the public can take to protect their health when pollutants reach unhealthy concentrations. The AQI focuses on health effects that can happen within a few hours or days after breathing polluted air.

- **"Sunwise"** was developed several years ago to educate and inform communities about ozone depletion and its adverse effects on the environment and health. It includes an overview of ozone depletion, its causes, and what we can do to address the issue. Its primary focus is on preventing or minimizing adverse health effects.

- **Air Quality Trends "Fact Book" and Website** (http://www.epa.gov/air/airtrends). Shows air quality trends in metropolitan areas using the latest data.

- **Tier 2 Brochure** Tier 2/Gasoline Sulfur Brochure ("Refineries and Cleaner Fuels: reducing sulfur to improve the air"). OAR has developed a brochure designed to educate communities living around refineries. The brochure describes the environmental benefits of the Tier 2/gasoline sulfur program, why refineries may need to get permits to make changes needed to reduce gasoline sulfur levels, and how community members can get involved in the permitting process.

- **It All Adds Up to Cleaner Air** (http://www.italladdsup.gov) is a unique public education and partnership-building initiative developed collaboratively by several federal agencies to help regional, state and community efforts to reduce traffic congestion and air pollution. It All Adds Up emphasizes simple, convenient actions people can take to improve air quality and reduce congestion. The voluntary initiative is sponsored by the U.S. Department of Transportation's (DOT) Federal Highway Administration, OAR's Office of Transportation and Air Quality, and DOT's Federal Transit Administration.

- **Mobile Source Outreach Assistance Competition.** Each year, OAR's Office of Transportation and Air Quality (OTAQ) manages a competition for state and local air agencies which is designed to provide "seed" funding for innovative outreach projects which can be replicated in like communities nationwide. Environmental Justice is one of the primary areas of emphasis in the annual Request for Proposal.

OAR has also consistently promoted, supported, and provided resources to enhance regional, state, and local environmental justice initiatives. Unlike the projects listed in **Section 4: Program Support**, OAR is not the lead for the projects listed below. However, OAR has decided to support these efforts to build relationships and to foster a collaborative atmosphere to more effectively achieve desired environmental results. OAR has found these efforts to be tremendously successful partnerships. Some examples are:

- **Environmental Justice Training Collaborative.** OAR continues to support efforts to centralize the continued implementation and further development of environmental justice training in the Agency.

- **Reducing Air Emissions at Airports.** Many of the nation's busiest airports are located in urban areas which struggle to meet air quality standards. EPA shares concerns about how airport-related emissions impact surrounding communities and recognizes the challenges that airport activities pose on state and local efforts to achieve and maintain healthy air quality. OAR is providing both technical support and financial resources to ensure that air emissions from airports are being properly addressed and reduced. OAR staff are currently participating as advisors for an activity appropriately characterized as a federal-city partnership to enhance the lives of the residents of Los Angeles. EPA has convened several interagency meetings to dialogue with organizations having responsibility, authority, and technical expertise concerning issues involving airport operations in order to develop the framework for a comprehensive study to determine the contribution of air emissions from Los Angeles World Airport (LAX) to the surrounding communities. However, airport-related environmental justice issues are not unique to Los Angeles; this study also provides the opportunity for Federal interagency cooperation to develop methodologies and guidance that could serve as a model for future studies throughout the country.

--- **Air Quality and Source Apportionment Study of the Area Surrounding Los Angeles International Airport**

The *Air Quality and Source Apportionment Study of the Area Surrounding LAX*, a technically complex, comprehensive study-- unprecedented in scope, involves numerous issues of great importance to EPA and would not only benefit stakeholders in the Los Angeles area, but would produce data to be used in future assessments at other airports nationwide. The air toxics component of the air emissions generated by airport-related activities is of particular importance in this proposed study, and the results would also better position EPA and other relevant agencies to respond constructively to airport-related health and environmental concerns expressed by communities throughout the country.

Components of the study plan including the Technical Workplan, Emission Inventory Protocol, Fuel Sampling Protocol, and Pilot Study Quality Assurance Project Plan have been developed in draft by consultants contracted by LAX with oversight and technical assistance provided by representatives of EPA, the California Air Resources Board, and South Coast Air Quality Management District. OAR staff are also providing guidance to LAX concerning development of a meaningful community involvement plan, formation of a public advisory committee, and related matters.

- **Maricopa County Risk Assessment**. This is a partnership between the three tribes located in the Phoenix area and the State of Arizona to identify and address air toxics risks. This project will also address environmental justice-related issues for both minority and disadvantaged communities within the Phoenix city limits.

Section 8: Data Collection, Management, and Evaluation

- List your Regional/Headquarters office's main data sets - the ways in which you collect environmental justice information. Also, describe how this information is utilized by your Regional/Headquarters office (e.g., environmental justice assessment, program tracking/evaluation, etc.).
- Does your Regional/Headquarters office have a method of identifying and highlighting best practices and lessons learned? If yes, please describe.

Traditionally, OAR does not collect environmental justice information in an isolated manner. However, there are a number of air quality-related data resources which this Office maintains and which are used to better characterize and assess the air quality in local communities. This information is also used to evaluate program effectiveness and to identify areas where additional attention may be needed.

The AirData Web site provides access to yearly summaries of United States air pollution data, taken from EPA's air pollution databases. The data include all fifty states in addition to the District of Columbia, Puerto Rico, and the U. S. Virgin Islands. AirData contains information about pollution sources and monitoring levels.

Air quality data can mainly be found in the AIRS, National Emissions Trends, and the National Emission Inventory for Hazardous Air Pollutants Databases. As a result of best practices and lessons learned, OAR:

- established a new cooperative agreement with the University of Michigan School of Public Health that will result in a broad review of community-based indoor environmental asthma interventions to determine the best and most effective practices in local communities around the country.

Section 9: Professional and Organizational Development

- Does your Regional/Headquarters office plan to provide training on environmental justice? If yes, please list and describe.

- What methods do you utilize to promote shared learning, such as best practices and lessons learned among staff? If yes, please list and describe.

OAR is offering voluntary training on the fundamentals of environmental justice to all of its staff on a periodic basis. Personnel involved in permitting, urban air toxic initiatives, community based initiatives, and those evaluating cumulative risk from toxic emissions are the primary target audience. To date, approximately 44 OAR staff have taken the training. OAR management believe this is an important training which can benefit all staff including OAR managers. OAR staff are also assisting the OEJ in providing the fundamentals course to other internal and external constituents.

In order to identify new methods to help promote shared learning and best practices in local communities, ORIA's Indoor Environments Division (IED) continues to fund a number of projects that are targeted at diverse and under served populations. The objective is to create a system for identifying new methods in a consistent and most effective manner. A important component of this approach is the contracting with Georgetown University's National Center for Cultural Competency to review IED's current program and to recommend strategies by which IED can enhance the impact of their outreach efforts to diverse and undeserved populations.

IED Cultural Competency Project. The Indoor Environments Division (IED) is contracting with Georgetown University's National Center for Cultural Competency to review IED's current program and to recommend strategies by which IED can enhance the impact of the Division's outreach efforts to diverse and underserved populations. Major activities of the initiative include the following:

- An overview session on cultural competency for all Division staff was completed. The session helped to provide a uniform understanding about the tenets of cultural competency.
- Focus group sessions have been conducted with each self-directed work team which helped to identify the issues the teams faced in working with specific populations. The sessions also helped the teams to streamline their respective goals in effectively reaching cultural diverse and socio-economically diverse populations.
- Outcomes of the focus group discussions were reviewed by team members.
- Follow up meetings have been scheduled with selected teams in the next few weeks to continue work on meeting their program goals. Examples of the programs of the teams are the urban schools initiative, implementation of Tools for Schools in urban areas, achieving indoor air quality risk reduction in racially, ethnically, and/or socio-economically diverse homes, etc.
- The cultural competency strategic plan will be ready for implementation in early 2004.

Section 10: Environmental Justice Assessment

- Does your Regional/Headquarters office have a process by which an environmental justice assessment is conducted? If yes, please describe.
- Does your Regional/Headquarters office rely on any information resources with which to conduct an environmental justice assessment, such as the Environmental Justice Mapper, Environmental Justice Toolkit, etc.? If yes, please list and describe.

To date, OAR's environmental justice assessments have generally consisted of a review of demographic data (including socioeconomic status, minority populations and educational background) and the generation of GIS maps of the area of impact.

Radiation Ambient Monitoring Systems (ERAMS) Project. This initiative (also entitled the National Radiation Monitoring Program) supports the provision of emergency response in the event of a large scale national incident (such as that of a Chernobyl or similar incident). Major goals of the initiative are to provide good baseline data and to generate good decision making data to help protect public health. Some specially selected sites, for example, with respect to tribes in Prairie Island, Minnesota have been in place for several years. These air sites help to provide ongoing special monitoring for tribal lands. The project is being implemented on population basis, whereby NAREL is adding air monitoring stations in many communities which include EJ-related communities.

Section 11: Program Evaluation

- Does your Regional/Headquarters office have any performance measures specifically related to environmental justice? If yes, please describe.

- Will your Regional/Headquarters office conduct any needs assessments, reports or other documents (produced internally or through a contract) to identify, quantify, and evaluate methods to strengthen and/or improve your environmental justice program? If yes, please list and describe.

Success with OAR Environmental Justice initiatives is measured by the extensive number of ongoing projects and their effectiveness in addressing far reaching issues which are critical to the environmental justice community. As mentioned earlier in this Action Plan, OAR plans to review progress on implementing the Environmental Justice Action Plan on a frequent basis. If OAR management determines that sufficient progress is not being made in a timely manner, a determination will be made on how to strengthen or improve the Office's performance.

Key personnel, with specific responsibility to coordinate environmental justice-related issues for the Office, have performance measures which are specifically related to environmental justice.

OFFICE OF AIR AND RADIATION
ENVIRONMENTAL JUSTICE
ACTION PLAN MATRIX

Goal - any of the 5 major goals identified in the EPA Strategic Plan FY 2006-2011 and the Cross Cutting Strategy.

Objectives - any of the 8 national environmental justice priorities or other priorities identified by the Headquarters Program Office or Region to accomplish a goal.

Activity - any action undertaken in order to address an Objective
Output - the direct results of an Activity. "Output measures" answer, quantitatively, the question: What will be accomplished under each activity?

Outcome - description of the impacts (*i.e.*, changes in condition) resulting from an Activity. "Outcome measures" answer the question: What impacts will the output/activities make relevant to public health and/or the environment.Short-term (awareness) – changes in learning, knowledge, attitude skills, understanding
  ▪ Intermediate (behavior) – changes in behavior, practice or decisions
  ▪ Long-term (condition) – changes in condition[1]

Point of Contact ("POC") - The main contact person for the specific activity.

---

[1] Office of Policy, Economics and Innovation. National Center for Environmental Innovation. Evaluation Support Division, "Introduction to Performance Measurement."

2007-2008 ORIA EJ Action Plan
(CY 2007-FY 2008)

Goal 1: Clean Air and Global Climate Change
Objective 1:   Reduction in number of asthma attacks (e.g., reduce asthma triggers such as particulate matter)

Activities	Output	Applicable Outcome Measure			Point of Contact
		Short-term (awareness)	Intermediate (behavior)	Long-term (condition)	
Support the Regional- Tribal Effective Asthma Management Project (TEAM) which is a program designed to increase tribal capability in assessing, understanding, and reduce exposure to environmental triggers of asthma. Recent asthma prevalence studies have shown some tribes within EPA Regions have asthma rates up to 2.5 times higher than the national average	The TEAM Project will respond to tribal needs with direct training, education that is culturally specific and designed to reduce the deleterious health impacts of asthma to Native American communities using a focused, systematic, multi-disciplinary asthma service, designed to coordinate and optimize the delivery of asthma care.	Increase awareness of at-risk populations by updating the Asthma Register - the Register is used to identify the patient population for asthma clinic services. The Asthma Register system is a component of the Indian Health Service resource and patient management system.	Increase the number of asthma action plans created; and the number of IAQ mitigations made in the home environment. Home visit referrals will be made to "survey" to determine if any asthma triggers are present and track clusters of occurrences.	Through training and education, adults and children with asthma, (particularly from tribal/underserved communities) will experience fewer asthma attacks and have improved quality of life and result in a decrease in the number of missed school days and in emergency room visits.	Chris Griffin Indoor Environments Division (IED) Tel: (202) 343-9421 E-mail: griffin.chris@epa.gov

Activities	Output	Applicable Outcome Measure			Point of Contact
		Short-term (awareness)	Intermediate (behavior)	Long-term (condition)	
Support partnership with Association of Clinicians for the Underserved (ACU) to work on reducing indoor asthma triggers for pediatric asthma patients by improving clinicians' ability to integrate the assessment of environmental factors into a comprehensive asthma management plan and standards of care. The ACU will target underserved communities which demonstrate the need for access to affordable, quality, transdisciplinary health care, and culturally-competent health care professionals. (Project and budget periods continue until 5/31/07)	By the end of the project in May 2007: Train 600 health care professionals on environmental management of asthma triggers. Complete curriculum on asthma and indoor air quality. The curriculum is continuously reviewed and improved to meet the cultural and special population needs of the audiences receiving this information.	Increased awareness of 600 primary care clinicians and health care teams who serve low-income, uninsured, under-insured, and culturally diverse patients.	An estimated increase of 25% of trained health care professionals will incorporate strategies for environmental management of indoor asthma triggers into clinical practice and standards of care for patients. The health care professionals will potentially impact an estimated 110,000 pediatric asthma patients in low-income, culturally-diverse communities.	Support EPA's Goal 1: Clean Air and Global Climate Change; Objective 1.2 Healthier Indoor Air; Sub-objective 1.1.1 – More People Breathing Cleaner Air. By 2012, 6.5 million people with asthma will be taking all essential actions to reduce exposures to their indoor asthma triggers (thereby preventing about 90,000 ER visits annually and producing other positive health outcomes.	David Rowson Indoor Environments Division (IED) Tel: (202) 343-9449 E-mail: rowson.david@epa.gov

3

Activities	Output	Applicable Outcome Measure			Point of Contact
		Short-term (awareness)	Intermediate (behavior)	Long-term (condition)	
Support partnership with U.S. Department of Health and Human Services Head Start Bureau to provide Early Head Start and Head Start grantees with education, training tools, and resources to help reduce children's health effects from environmental asthma triggers and secondhand smoke. Head Start programs provide comprehensive child development services to low-income families (including children from birth to five and pregnant women).	Conduct activities at national conferences and at regional Head Start centers which promote effective interventions for reduction of the health effects of secondhand smoke exposure environmental asthma triggers on young children. Activities will: (1) create and promote education materials; (2) increase access to EPA's websites, hotlines and other resources; (3) provide technical assistance; (4) track and share results	By December 2007, an increase of 2000 Head Start grantees and families with asthma will gain greater knowledge about ways to reduce the health risks from exposure to secondhand smoke and asthma triggers in their centers and home environments, as measured by post evaluations, home pledges, and clearinghouse orders.	By December 2007, Head Start centers and families representing 3,000 to 5,000 children will actively pledge to keep their homes and vehicles smoke-free and/or will maintain a management plan to reduce asthma triggers in their home environments, as measured by pre- and post- activity evaluations	By September 2008, the health risk from exposure to secondhand smoke and asthma triggers will be reduced in Head Start programs representing combined enrollments totaling 10,000 children through smoke-free homes or in maintaining an active asthma management plan (as measured by reports from participating Head Start grantees).	Mike Holloway Indoor Environments Division (IED) Tel: (202) 343-9426 E-mail: holloway.mike@epa.go v

4

Activities	Output	Applicable Outcome Measure			Point of Contact
		Short-term (awareness)	Intermediate (behavior)	Long-term (condition)	
Childhood Asthma Public Service Campaign Implement "Goldfish" childhood asthma media campaign targeted to parents from underserved communities (i.e. low-income, under-represented, and medically-underserved families) and inner-city pediatric asthma patients. The media campaign is designed to raise awareness about asthma and generate behavior change toward the management of childhood asthma.	Conduct 2-3 regional media training events for community coalitions and community asthma programs. Distribute campaign materials to media markets serving urban populations and distribute campaign materials to media markets serving Hispanic and Tribal populations.	Increase awareness in the number of parents of children with asthma and their capability to manage asthma triggers at home as measured by: a) Goldfish media campaign awareness at or above 20 %; b) additional 250,000 unique web hits (www.noattacks.org) c) increase in donated media time for Goldfish campaign; d) two communities will localize the media campaign	As a result of the Childhood Asthma Public Service Campaign, more parents caring for children with asthma are taking more action to manage their child's triggers and reduce attacks.	Children with asthma will experience fewer asthma attacks and have improved quality of life.	David Rowson Indoor Environments Division (IED) Tel: (202) 343-9449 E-mail: rowson.david@epa.gov

5

Activities	Output	Applicable Outcome Measure			Point of Contact
		Short-term (awareness)	Intermediate (behavior)	Long-term (condition)	
Communities in Action for Asthma Friendly Environments Initiative Implement a two day Asthma Forum. Develop communication and outreach tools to promote the Forum, recruit participants (particularly from programs providing care to low-income, under-represented, and other medically underserved communities), manage logistics and conduct follow-up with attendees. Support on-line Network of Communities to foster real time learning and information exchange. Implement a national awards program highlighting outstanding programs providing quality care to underserved groups.	1) Implement a Forum event in Washington, DC (May 31-June 1, 2007) 2) Support the Asthma Community on-line Network by hosting web site, marketing, training, and educational opportunities through the Network, and posting unique tools and resources. 3) Recognize quality care efforts through national awards program.	Representatives of 100 community based asthma programs will have increased knowledge and take action to reduce exposure to environmental asthma triggers in communities disproportionately impacted by asthma. Up to 4 community programs serving people with asthma, will deliver quality asthma care as benchmarked by Exemplary Award criteria.	100 community-based asthma programs participating in *Communities in Action for Asthma Friendly Environments* Initiative will deliver quality asthma care, and improving asthma outcomes for those they serve., as measured by the number of participating communities	Adults and children with asthma, (particularly from low-income, under-represented, and other medically underserved communities) will experience fewer asthma attacks and have improved quality of life.	David Rowson Indoor Environments Division (IED) Tel: (202) 343-9449 E-mail: rowson.david@epa.gov

| Activities | Output | Applicable Outcome Measure | | | Point of Contact |
		Short-term (awareness)	Intermediate (behavior)	Long-term (condition)	
Support the partnership with the Aberdeen Area Tribal Chairmen's Health Board to collaborate with multiple partners within and across regional boundaries in order to provide environmental asthma trigger management education and to promote the capability and development of tribal healthcare professionals to assist their patients identify and mitigate asthma triggers in the home. (Project and budget periods continue until 09/30/07)	By the end of the project in September, 2007, Aberdeen's Board will implement a Tribal Asthma Prevention Campaign which provides education on the management and prevention of environmental asthma triggers to a population of almost 200,000 tribal members residing on seventeen reservations and in two urban Indian service areas in North Dakota, South Dakota, Nebraska, and Iowa.	By the end of year two, the activity will increase awareness and education by merging evidenced-based practices with culturally-competent approaches. In addition, increased knowledge of in-home asthma triggers and methods of trigger mitigation among American Indian tribal members and health professionals.	By the end of year three, an increased number of healthcare programs will commit to conducting in-home asthma assessments, as evidenced by a 25% increase in the rate of in-home assessments conducted by healthcare programs.	This project will contribute to EPA's strategic goal: by 2012; 6.5 million people with asthma will be taking all essential actions to reduce exposures to their indoor asthma triggers (thereby preventing about 90,000 ER visits annually and producing other positive health outcomes.	Chris Griffin Indoor Environments Division (IED) Tel: (202) 343-9421 E-mail: griffin.chris@epa.gov

Office of Radiation and Indoor Air
(CY2007-FY2008)

Goal 1: Clean Air and Global Climate Change
Objective 2: Reduce exposure to air toxics (e.g., reduce releases of mercury)

Activities	Output	Applicable Outcome Measure			Point of Contact
		Short-term (awareness)	Intermediate (behavior)	Long-term (condition)	
Support the partnership to increase the capability of Tribal Nation representatives to address various environmental health and other concerns on federally-recognized tribal lands (i.e. the capability to develop and implement air monitoring networks). This activity will be implemented in partnership with OAQPS and will continue providing technical training through the Tribal Air Monitoring (TAMS) Center.	Deliver 10 air monitoring training courses to approximately 100 tribal air professionals. Course topics include: particulate matter (PM), quality assurance project plans, data management, ozone, meteorological stations, air toxics, PM related databases and radiation. Provide direct technical assistance via equipment loans and gravimetric laboratory services.	Increase awareness in: (a) designing and implementing appropriate air monitoring networks, (b) improving data quality and, (c) improving ability to include air data in EPA national databases. Also, assure that air professionals are properly trained in network planning, data handling, quality assurance, and technical implementation.	Assist tribal representatives in implementing air monitoring networks that provide high quality data. Assist in building the capability to provide this data to EPA's air quality databases such that tribal air data that is used to implement tribal implementation plans for improving air quality.	By 2010, improve air quality in an additional 50 tribal communities by assisting the tribes, via training, to implement air monitoring networks and have this data included in EPA's air quality databases	Emilio Braganza Radiation & Indoor Environments National Laboratory (R&IE) Tel : 702-784-8280 Email : braganza.emilio@epa.gov

Activities	Output	Applicable Outcome Measure			Point of Contact
		Short-term (awareness)	Intermediate (behavior)	Long-term (condition)	
(1) Continue support of indoor radon testing by providing radon test kits and analysis within residences in economically-disadvantaged communities (2) Support the Erie County (NY)Tribal Community – Toxics Air Pollutants Project (Project and budget periods continue until 09/30/07)	Provide no-cost home radon test kits and analysis from the EPA R&IE Laboratory to partner groups and organizations (i.e. Tribes, nonprofit organizations, and national coalitions) that work directly with residents from low-income and/or tribal communities.	Increase awareness of indoor radon exposure risk by providing radon EPA test kits and analysis for low-income and/or tribal populations. Radon testing and analysis support gets underway within one week of the initial request.	Increase the number of residents actively taking appropriate action to reduce elevated radon levels by providing test results to partner groups and organizations that ultimately meet and provide follow-up education directly to the target audience.	By 2008, reduce lung cancer risks associated with exposure to elevated radon levels through increased awareness and action in the number of low-income and/or tribal homes. Increase the number of partner groups and organizations working within economically-disadvantaged and/or tribal homes by an additional 20-40% (as measured by number and source of test kit requests. Baseline: 1471 homes).	Evelyn Clay Radiation and Indoor Environments national Laboratory (R&IE) Tel: 702-798-2324 E-mail: clay.evelyn@epa.gov

9

Activities	Output	Applicable Outcome Measure			Point of Contact
		Short-term (awareness)	Intermediate (behavior)	Long-term (condition)	
Support the development and implementation of a 2007 Navajo Tribal Workshop designed to build the capacity of Navajo Nation representatives to address protection from exposures to uranium mine wastes on Navajo lands. Uranium mine wastes result in direct exposures to radiation and radon (including indoor environment exposure) throughout the reservation.	This activity will: a) identify steps and establish radiation protection standards; b) develop culturally-effective approaches toward planning and securing funding for surveying, decontaminating, and rebuilding houses constructed with radioactive uranium mine waste; c) identify ways in which EPA could assist in lessening impacts of abandoned uranium mines and; d) plan for additional culturally-appropriate educational materials for adults on uranium and radiation protection basics in Navajo and English languages.	As a result of the workshop: 1) a proposed schedule will be developed with responsible parties identified on the steps needed to establish radiation protection standards for the reservation; 2) a plan will be developed on how the Navajo agencies and EPA will work together to survey and alleviate problems associated with houses constructed with uranium mine waste; and 3) comments will have been provided to EPA on how to assist in lessening impacts of abandoned uranium mines.	By the end of 2008, the Navajo Nation will participate in: (a) establishing radiation protection standards for the reservation and; (b) developing a proposed schedule for surveying homes constructed with uranium mine wastes; (c) identifying responsible parties for locating funding sources and procedures to mitigate financial and other issues; and (d) providing input to EPA to formulate its planning on projects to lessen impacts of abandoned uranium mines.	By end of 2010, the Navajo Nation and EPA will help reduce health and environmental impacts of abandoned uranium mines on Tribal members as measured by the: (1) Tribe's establishment of radiation protection standards, and planning for surveys and remediation of contaminated houses; (2) completion of educational materials for adult members of the Tribe on uranium and radiation protection basics. The success of this effort will be measured by the number of follow-up activities for surveying and successfully remediating houses	Loren Setlow Radiation Protection Division Tel: 202-343-9445 E-mail: setlow.loren@epa.go v

10

Activities	Output	Applicable Outcome Measure			Point of Contact
		Short-term (awareness)	Intermediate (behavior)	Long-term (condition)	
Prepare the public access portion of RadNet data in bilingual Spanish/English language format. This activity will target audiences with limited English proficiency.	This activity will provide public access of information to residents with limited English proficiency about ambient and incident levels of airborne radioactive material. Bilingual information will be available to both Spanish and English speaking citizens.	A higher percentage of the general public will be informed about potential radiation risks and educated on background radiation levels.	N/A	The health risks associated with ambient and incident levels of airborne radioactive material will be reduced to both Spanish and English speaking citizens, as measured by information request.	Rhonda Sears National Air and Radiation Environmental Laboratory (NAREL) 334-270-3413 Sears.Rhonda @epa.gov

11

Activities	Output	Short-term (awareness)	Intermediate (behavior)	Long-term (condition)	Point of Contact
Support partnership with Wake Forest University School of Medicine (WFUSM) and the East Coast Migrant Head Start Program (ECMHSP) to train health educators to work with families of migrant farm workers to increase their knowledge and change behaviors that will reduce the impact of secondhand smoke related disease among children in the ECMHSP Head Start centers. The ECMHSP Head Start centers are located in eleven states along the east coast and services approximately 8,500 infants, toddlers and preschoolers. (Budget and Project Periods continue until 9/30/09)	Complete six Focus Groups with a total of ninety participants. Develop educational materials for ECMHSP core staff, teachers, and parents. Implement training program. Provide Train-the-Trainer module to ECMHSP staff at 50 Centers. In turn, staff will train teachers and parents and all will incorporate an educational, outreach, and training program aimed at reducing the risk of exposure to residential indoor air pollution among Head Start children.	Increased awareness among ECMHSP core staff, teachers and parents. The program would become part of ECMHSP's standard staff training and standard health disability services coordinator health programs. *Baseline: Estimates of baseline from data provided by ECMHSP for* *2005 - 0% of core staff, teachers, and parents trained in residential ETS. Because it is possible that some core staff and teachers will have obtained training in environmental health prior to program start, updated data will be obtained.*	An estimated increase of 30% of parents will more knowledge on the dangers of secondhand smoke exposure to children; (2) more knowledge on ways to prevent secondhand smoke exposure to children and; (3) actively commit to creating a smoke-free environment for their children.	By 2012, reduce the percent of low-income and minority children aged 6 and under regularly exposed to secondhand smoke in the home to be equivalent with rates in the general population (estimated to be 11% in 2003)	Sheila Brown Indoor Environments Division (IED) Tel: (202) 343-9439 E-mail: brown.sheila@epa.go v

12

Activities	Output	Applicable Outcome Measure			Point of Contact
		Short-term (awareness)	Intermediate (behavior)	Long-term (condition)	
CET will collaborate with health care professionals and social service providers to educate parents (especially new mothers from low-income or economically-disadvantaged backgrounds) to protect their children from environmental tobacco smoke (ETS) exposure and potentially reduce the incidence of asthma through prevention, education, training, and outreach. CET will provide environmental health assessment training to health care professionals on how to assess homes and lifestyles for ETS risks. The health care professionals will counsel parents about practical approaches to reduce their children's risks to ETS exposure.

Budget and budget periods continue until 9/30/09. | CET will develop an environmental health assessment tool, educational materials, and resource books.

CET will train nurses, other health care professionals and social service providers on how to use the environmental health assessment tool to access and counsel parents and caregivers on behaviors and lifestyles that can reduce their children's incidence of exposure to ETS and asthma episodes. | Increase awareness of health care professionals and social service providers on how to assess homes and lifestyles for ETS risks and how to counsel parents on practical approaches to reduce their children's risks from ETS exposure. | Nurses, health care professionals and social service providers will provide ETS management education, training, and outreach to over 600 families utilizing the environmental health assessment and other resources provided. | Reduce the percentage of low-income and/or minority children (aged 6 and under) who are regularly exposed to health risks associated with secondhand smoke in their homes.

Increase (by 30%) parental knowledge on (a) children's health risks to ETS; (b) ways to prevent exposure to children and; (c) creating a smoke-free environment for their children. | Sheila Brown Indoor Environments Division (IED) Tel: (202) 343-9439

E-mail: brown.sheila@epa.go v |

Activities	Output	Applicable Outcome Measure			Point of Contact
		Short-term (awareness)	Intermediate (behavior)	Long-term (condition)	
Support partnership with the Inter-Tribal Council of Michigan (ITCM) to develop and implement environmental tobacco smoke (ETS) training materials, program curriculum and assessment tools in accordance with current EPA materials. (Project and budget periods continue until 09/30/07)	The project will make accessible outreach materials and tools that are designed to train parents and caregivers of children enrolled in Tribal Head Start programs (including Head Start staff) on the dangers of ETS by providing specific and culturally-competent ETS-related information	By the end of year two, increase (by 75%) the number of parents and caregivers of children enrolled in the Tribal Head Start programs with knowledge of the dangers of environmental tobacco smoke in each of the eight tribal communities, as measured by training agendas and pre/post assessments.	By the end of year three, increase (by 25%) the percentage of Head Start parents who implement new smoke-free homes policies, within the eight tribal communities, as measured by post follow up Head Start parent assessments.	By the end of the project period in September 2007, the project will reduce the total number of children regularly exposed to environmental tobacco smoke, within the Native American homes of eight tribal communities.	Chris Griffin Indoor Environments Division (IED) Tel: (202) 343-9421 E-mail: griffin.chris@epa.gov

14

Office of Radiation and Indoor Air
(CY2007-FY2008)

Goal 4: Healthy Communities and Ecosystems
Objective 2: Collaborative problem-solving to address environmental justice issues

Activities	Output	Applicable Outcome Measure			Point of Contact
		Short-term (awareness)	Intermediate (behavior)	Long-term (condition)	
Build knowledge and capability of tribal representatives on indoor air health risk reduction through providing hands-on indoor air training to tribal environmental professionals and by working cooperatively with nonprofit partners including the American Lung Association of Minnesota and Northern Arizona University's Institute for Tribal Environmental Professionals (ITEP).	Deliver 11 courses in FY04-FY08 to increase capability in targeting ASHRAE climatic zones. Courses focus on 1) investigating indoor air problems in homes and building science; 2) remediation and; 3) establishing an IAQ program. Training will be for approximately 220 environmental professionals.	Build tribal knowledge and awareness of IAQ health related issues through hands-on training. Provide two Tech I/II courses in Hot and Hot/Humid climates in FY07.	Provide environmental professionals with the resources and training to develop, implement, and maintain an IAQ program within tribal communities, thereby enabling them to determine the level of contamination and remediation which may be required.	By 2008, reduce indoor air quality (IAQ) health risks in tribal communities by increasing the number of individuals trained and educated on assessing and remediating IAQ problems in homes, and increasing the number of IAQ community programs. (No baseline identified)	Alejandra Baer Radiation and Indoor Environments National Laboratory (R&IE) Tel: 702-784-8281 E-mail: baer.alejandra@epa.gov

15

Goal 1: Clean Air and Global Climate Change
Objective 1:   Reduction in number of asthma attacks (e.g., reduce asthma triggers such as particulate matter)

Activities	Output	Applicable Outcome Measure			Point of Contact
		Short-term (awareness)	Intermediate (behavior)	Long-term(condition)	
Provide regulatory mechanism and implement permit programs for minor stationary sources located in Indian country or for major sources located in areas of Indian country not attaining the National Ambient Air Quality Standards (NAAQS)	Promulgate proposed and final Tribal/New Source Review (NSR) permit rules Design, conduct and evaluate permit training for permit writers on final rule Design, conduct, and evaluate Webex training for all Regions Tribes will develop and implement permit program Tribes will issue permits A level playing field for sources located in Indian country because the rule addresses significant regulatory gaps	In FY 07-08, EPA will have published both proposed and final rules In FY 07-08, conduct training in Regions 8,9, and 10 In FY 07-08, conduct Webex training for all Regions Increase knowledge of NSR permitting process	In FY 07-08, Regional offices and Tribes issue permits in a timely manner consistent with regulations Industry complies with permits Number % of NSR permits in Indian country reporting compliance Assist with policy and technical questions	Provide level playing field for Tribes to attract industry while maintaining/improving air quality in Indian country.	Jessica Montanez (919) 541-3407

Goal 1: Clean Air and Global Climate Change
Objective 2:   Reduce exposure to air toxics (e.g., reduce releases of mercury)

Activities	Output	Applicable Outcome Measure			Point of Contact
		Short-term (awareness)	Intermediate (behavior)	Long-term (condition)	
Help all communities to live in a healthy environment, while accomplishing goals set forth in OAR's Urban Air Toxics Strategy	Provide information and guidance to the Regions and communities on key categories particularly the Autobody Shop Campaign. Develop and maintain tools for the Community Program	Raise communities awareness by tracking the number of brochures, notebooks and hits on website	Ten communities to Adopt Autobody Pilot Program	Track reductions in hazard air pollutants (HAP) from the Autobody Campaign	Holly Wilson 919-541-5624

17

Goal 1: Clean Air and Global Climate Change
Objective 2:   Reduce exposure to air toxics (e.g., reduce releases of mercury)

Activities	Output	Applicable Outcome Measure			Point of Contact
		Short-term (awareness)	Intermediate (behavior)	Long-term (condition)	
While collaborating with Tribal air officials design a 'Great American Woodstove Changeout and Burn Clean Campaign' for Indian country using principles learned from other wood smoke reduction efforts, (e.g. Libby Montana Campaign, Oneida Tribe, Nez Perce Study) 2006-2007	Work with tribes, other EPA offices like HUD, BIA, DOE to reduce exposure of residential wood smoke (toxics and PM) indoors and out through collaborative process	By March 2007, form a Tribal Wood Smoke Workgroup to develop outreach materials and lessons learned from other efforts like Libby, Montana woodstove change out champaign and Nez Perce study Track workgroup progress, number of meetings, & timelines	By 2008, develop tribal wood smoke outreach and educational materials Track number of materials distributed and people reached	Continuously track the number of households changed-out to cleaner burning hearth appliances Track tons of emissions reduced	Larry Brockman 919-541-5398

18

Office of Air Quality Planning and Standards
(CY2007-FY2008)

Goal 1: Clean Air and Global Climate Change
Objective 2: *Reduce exposure to air toxics (e.g., reduce releases of mercury)*

Activities	Output	Applicable Outcome Measure			Point of Contact
		Short-term (awareness)	**Intermediate (behavior)**	**Long-term (condition)**	
Identify and determine the additional capabilities required to enhance and refine BenMap or other resources to more accurately perform impact analysis	Incorporate distributional analysis into the rulemaking process for selected regulations	Add additional demographic variables to BenMAP software and test using PM NAAQS RIA input data (6 months)	Analyze projected air quality impacts and associated distributions for selected OAQPS regulations (1 year)	Based on criteria and design specifications provided by the OAQPS EJ team, develop an EJ screening tool. Estimate need one year to test, validate and distribute screening tool after design specs agreed to	Lillian Bradley (919) 541-5694

Office of Air Quality Planning and Standards
(CY2007-FY2008)

Goal 1: Clean Air and Global Climate Change :
Objective 2: Reduce exposure to air toxics (e.g., reduce releases of mercury)

Activities	Output	Applicable Outcome Measure			Point of Contact
		Short-term (awareness)	Intermediate (behavior)	Long-term (condition)	
Develop and deliver national conference/training on best practices with respect to environmental justice and air issues	National conference on best practices (FY 07)	Increase capacity of communities and other stakeholders to identify and use best practices to address environmental justice issues, as measured by attendees satisfaction survey	Communities and other stakeholders use best practices identified at conference, as measured by post-conference survey	Increase capacity of communities and other stakeholders to develop effective programs and strategies to address EJ issues	Candace Carraway (919) 541-3189
Develop and deliver national workshop on federal permit programs to community advocates and other stakeholders	Deliver national workshop on federal permit programs	Improve understanding of permit procedures and complex issues, as measured by attendees satisfaction survey	Attendees use workshop information to improve comments and participation in permit programs, as measured by post-training survey	Improved quality of comments on permits	

Goal 1: Clean Air and Global Climate Change
Objective 3:   Reduce exposure to air toxics

Activities	Output	Applicable Outcome Measure			Point of Contact
		Short-term (awareness)	Intermediate (behavior)	Long-term (condition)	
Continue to implement a risk-based air toxics program for stationary sources	Continued development of area sources rules Provide support to regional offices and others to ensure that promulgated emission standards are effectively implemented by developing implementation tools Continued development of residual risk rules Rules reflect the EJ policies and objectives as much as practicable Develop a methodology (as resources allow) for EJ analysis for (MACT) and residual risk	Complete five residual risk rules and began implementing a methodology to streamline the rule development process for the remaining categories, which will consolidate many categories in a single regulatory action	Begin developing a methodology for completing area source rules for 50 source categories over the next three years Begin developing rules for four area source categories. Apply EJ analytical techniques and tools as available and applicable	When fully implemented (by 2008), maximum achievable control technology (MACT) standards covering 174 source categories will result in air toxics emission reductions of 1.7 million tons/year	John Bosch (919) 541-5583 David Solomon (919) 541-5375

21

Goal 4: Healthy Communities and Ecosystems
Objective 2:   Collaborative problem-solving to address environmental justice issues

Activities	Output	Applicable Outcome Measure			Point of Contact
		Short-term (awareness)	**Intermediate** (behavior)	**Long-term** (condition)	
Support the efforts of Regions and States in identifying areas of the country that do not attain the new 24-hour PM2.5 NAAQS	Provide information on air quality and the designations process to Regions, States, and Tribes	In FY-07-08 provide guidance and outreach to Regions, States, and Tribes	Assess effectiveness of outreach materials and Regional efforts at informing affected communities	Designations guidance to States and Tribes by Spring, 2007	Kimber Scavo (919) 541-3354 Julie McClintock (919) 541-5339 Amy Vasu (919) 541-0107 Rich Damberg (919) 541-5592
Provide direct support to tribal governments in assessing attainment with the new 24-hour PM2.5 NAAQS		Track materials developed and distributed			

Office of Air Quality Planning and Standards
(CY 2007-FY 2008)

Goal 4: Healthy Communities and Ecosystems
Objective 2:   Collaborative problem-solving to address environmental justice issues

Activities	Output	Applicable Outcome Measure			Point of Contact
		Short-term (awareness)	Intermediate (behavior)	Long-term (condition)	
Support Regional and State efforts to engage disproportionately affected communities in the development of State Implementation Plan (SIP) for ozone, particulate matter and Regional Haze	Provide requested support to Regions and States as they assist disproportionately affected communities	Provide requested guidance and outreach to Regions and States	Assess value and effectiveness of trainings	Increased capacity of Tribal governments to participate in SIP process.	Julie McClintock (919) 541-5339

Kimber Scavo (919) 541-3354

Rhea Jones (919) 541-2940 |
| | Improve technical capacity of Tribes to assess off-reservation sources | In FY07, conduct two tribal trainings | | | |
| Work with Regions to support tribal governments in effectively participating in development of SIPs | Increase effectiveness of tribal participation in state planning processes, and continue building and strengthening relationships with state and local agencies | Offer training workshop in March, 2007 focusing on Region 8 and 10 tribal air quality concerns

Track number of people trained | | | |

Goal 4: Healthy Communities and Ecosystems
Objective 2: Collaborative problem-solving to address environmental justice issues

Activities	Output	Applicable Outcome Measure			Point of Contact
		Short-term (awareness)	Intermediate (behavior)	Long-term (condition)	
Implementation of the Memorandum of Understanding with North Carolina Agricultural and Technical State University (NC A&T SU)	EPA will visit NC A&T SU twice per year to provide information to students about careers at EPA	Increase awareness of environmental careers to NC A&T SU students	Increase the number of students from NC A&T SU who can articulate various environmentally related career opportunities	Increase the number of NC A&T SU students who seek, get offered, and accept employment with EPA	Phyllis Wright (919) 541-5369
Provide students with information about careers at EPA	EPA will offer 2 to 3 lectures per year to NC A&T SU classes on various environmental issues, including environmental justice specifically	Increase awareness of environmental issues, including environmental justice, to students at NC A&T SU	Increase the number of students at NC A&T SU who can comprehensively articulate various environmental issues.		
Provide support to the university staff	EPA will provide internship opportunities to 10-15 NC A&T SU students per year	Increase awareness of EPA, its mission, and the mission of the Office of Air Quality Planning and Standards (OAQPS) to students at NC A&T SU	Increase the number of students at NC A&T SU who can comprehensively articulate the EPA mission and the mission of OAQPS		
Provide learning opportunities to students through the annual intern program					

24

Goal 4: Healthy Communities and Ecosystems
Objective 2:   Collaborative problem-solving to address environmental justice issues

Activities	Output	Applicable Outcome Measure			Point of Contact
		Short-term (awareness)	Intermediate (behavior)	Long-term (condition)	
As areas with potential EJ concerns are identified, provide a mechanism for identifying areas/cities/towns /counties violating NAAQS	Advise and review state/local decisions on monitor placement under EPA regulations and produce and update list of air quality conditions in the US where potential EJ concerns exist	Increase public awareness of adverse air quality areas with potential EJ concerns. The most current air quality Information can be found at www.epa.gov/air/oaqps/greenbk Track number off website hits	Increased focus on managing air quality in areas with potential EJ concerns.	The health risk from exposure to unhealthy levels of air pollution will be reduced (as measured by increased number of areas attaining the NAAQS).	Tom Helms (919) 541-5527

Office of Air Quality Planning Standards
(CY2007-FY2008)

Cross Cutting Strategies:
Objective: Internal Capacity Building (e.g., internal program management)

Activities	Output	Applicable Outcome Measure			Point of Contact
		Short-term (awareness)	Intermediate (behavior)	Long-term (condition)	
Develop OAQPS policy on environmental justice Develop guidance and training for OAQPS rulewriters on compliance with EO 12898 and OAQPS EJ policy	OAQPS policy on environmental justice (FY 07) In FY 07, develop initial screening tool to identify rules that require an EJ analysis In FY 08, develop tool kit for EJ analyses, including enhanced public involvement In FY 08, develop and deliver training for OAQPS rulewriters	Increase awareness of OAQPS staff and managers regarding content of EJ policy, as measured by number of employees trained via briefings Increase awareness of OAQPS staff and managers regarding procedures and tools for EJ analyses, as measured by pre-and post training surveys	Staff applies screening to all rulemaking actions, and for rules that raise environmental justice concerns, OAQPS rulewriters identify and address EJ using toolkit, as measured by number of rules that consider EJ implications	Increased capacity to evaluate EJ issues and adopt appropriate options for public involvement and avoidance or mitigation of disproportionate adverse environmental and health consequences.	Candace Carraway 919-541-3189

26

**Office of Air Quality Planning Standards
(CY2007-FY2008)**

Cross Cutting Strategies:
Objective: Internal Capacity Building (e.g., internal program management)

Activities	Output	Applicable Outcome Measure			Point of Contact
		Short-term (awareness)	Intermediate (behavior)	Long-term (condition)	
Develop environmental justice training tailored for OAQPS employees	Present EJ training for OAQPS employees	Increased awareness of OAQPS staff and managers regarding EJ policy and as measured by pre-and post training surveys	Integration of OAQPS EJ policy and affected community perspectives into analysis of new and existing projects, as measured by post workshop survey (%/# of attendees reporting consideration of how to integrate EJ into their work)		Candace Carraway 919-541-3189

Office of Atmospheric Programs
(CY2007-FY2008)

Goal 1: Clean Air and Global Climate Change
Objective 1.1   Healthier Outdoor Air, Ozone and PM₂.₅ (e.g., reduce asthma triggers such as particulate matter)

Activities	Output	Outcome			Contact
		Short-term	Intermediate	Long-term	
Development of Clean Air Interstate Rule (CAIR) Environmental Justice Assessment	Building on existing staff analysis of the environmental justice impacts of the Acid Rain Program, develop the format and analytical questions to periodically assess the impact of CAIR (implementation starting in 2010) on EJ communities.	One or more assessment concepts to present and evaluate available data on emissions, air quality, and/or health effects of SO_2, NO_x, and or $PM_{2.5}$ emissions from power plants on EJ communities.	NA	These analyses will be periodically included in our program progress reports.	Rick Haeuber, Chief Assessment and Communications Branch (202) 343-9250 haeuber.richard@epa.gov
Continue to implement the Acid Rain Program (ARP) SO_2 program	By 2011, reduce national annual emissions of sulfur dioxide (SO_2) from utility electrical power generation sources by approximately 8.45 million tons from the 1980 level of 17.4 million tons, achieving and maintaining the Acid Rain statutory SO_2 emissions cap of 8.95 million tons.	NA	NA	Analysis has shown that all people, regardless of race, color, national origin or income benefit from the Acid Rain Program. Continuing to implement the ARP SO_2 Program will reduce emissions of pollutants that form fine particles and cause human health problems for many communities, including environmental justice communities.	Rick Haeuber, Chief Assessment and Communications Branch (202) 343-9250 Haeuber.richard@epa.gov

Activities	Output	Outcome			Contact
		Short-term	Intermediate	Long-term	
Continue to implement the NO$_x$ Budget Trading Program (NBP) and NO$_x$ SIP Call	By 2011, reduce total annual average nitrogen deposition and mean total ambient nitrate concentration by 15 percent from 1990 monitored levels of up to 11 kilograms per hectare for total nitrogen deposition and 4.0 micrograms per cubic meter for mean total ambient nitrate concentration.	NA	NA	Continuing to implement the NBP and NO$_x$ SIP Call will reduce emissions of pollutants that form fine particles and ozone which cause human health problems for many communities, including environmental justice communities.	Rick Haeuber, Chief Assessment and Communications Branch (202) 343-9250 Haeuber.richard@epa.gov
Provide Spanish language information on the CAMD website	Translate portions of the CAMD website, currently being updated, into Spanish.	NA	NA	Translating informational portions of the updated website into Spanish will broaden access to the data and background on acid rain, air quality, health and ecological benefits, as well as information on cap and trade programs and current and future regulations.	Janice Wagner, Chief Market Operations Branch (202) 343-9118 Wagner.janice@epa.gov
Data and Maps website and databases	The Clean Air Markets Division's Data and Maps website is a publicly accessible portal to a variety of data including national power plant information, acid deposition and air quality data, and emissions and allowance data to query and download by a particular source, state and time period. Maintain Data and Maps website and the several databases housed within.	NA	NA	Access to the data in the Data and Maps portal is free and allows all people to better understand the air quality and emissions data in their communities.	Janice Wagner, Chief Market Operations Branch (202) 343-9118 Wagner.janice@epa.gov

29

Goal 1: Clean Air and Global Climate Change
Objective 1.3   Protect the Ozone Layer

Activities	Output	Outcome			Point of Contact
		Short-term	Intermediate	Long-term	
Promote ENERGY STAR residential new construction guidelines to affordable housing stakeholders	More state housing finance authorities will award points in the competitive grants process to housing projects that include an energy efficiency component. States that currently offer points for efficiency components will increase their level of commitment to efficiency in new, state-funded affordable housing projects. More HUD grantees will be aware of ENERGY STAR for new homes and add ENERGY STAR as a voluntary component to their HUD grant application requirements	More state housing authorities will recognize energy efficiency as a desirable component of new affordable housing.	NA	In the long term, more efficient affordable housing projects will be constructed, resulting in greater comfort and income savings for residents and reduced energy consumption.	David Lee, Chief ENERGY STAR Residential Branch (202) 343-9131 Lee.davidf@epa.gov

Activities	Output	Outcome			Point of Contact
		Short-term	Intermediate	Long-term	
Home Performance with ENERGY STAR	More owners of affordable housing units will have access to energy efficiency services and products, especially those who aren't poor enough to qualify for weatherization services and aren't wealthy enough to purchase efficiency services and products on the open market.	More affordable housing stakeholders such as state housing authorities and community development corporations will recognize energy efficiency as a desirable and necessary component of existing affordable housing.	NA	In the long term, more owners of existing affordable housing units will use energy efficiency services, resulting in greater comfort and income savings for residents and reduced energy consumption.	David Lee, Chief ENERGY STAR Residential Branch (202) 343-9131 Lee.davidf@epa.gov
Promote energy efficiency financing	More low income homeowners and renters will be able to secure funding (loans, grants, rebates, etc.) for efficiency improvements	Greater access to energy efficiency financing products for low-income homeowners and renters, leading to greater energy efficiency and increased housing affordability.	NA	In long term, existing homes will be retrofitted to be more efficient, resulting in greater comfort and income savings for residents and reduced energy consumption.	David Lee, Chief ENERGY STAR Residential Branch (202) 343-9131 Lee.davidf@epa.gov
ENERGY STAR construction guidelines for manufactured housing	The production and sale of more ENERGY STAR qualified manufactured homes	NA	NA	More energy efficient manufactured homes means lower-income homebuyers have greater access to efficient homes	David Lee, Chief ENERGY STAR Residential Branch (202) 343-9131 Lee.davidf@epa.gov

31

Activities	Output	Outcome			Point of Contact
		Short-term	Intermediate	Long-term	
Re-translation of the SunWise Program Tool Kit into Spanish	The SunWise Tool Kit is an educational curriculum aligned with national education standards that has been adopted by more than 14,000 schools and provides sun protection information to protect school children from excessive UV exposure and cancer risk. The Spanish version was last printed in 2002. Since that time, the English version of the Kit has been updated. Through this activity, the Kit would be re-translated into Spanish so it includes the updated material found in the English Kit.	More activities will be provided in Spanish, and facts will be updated from 2002, increasing awareness of the importance of sun protection among Spanish speakers.	NA	Reduced exposure to UV radiation	Ross Brennan, Chief Stratospheric Program Implementation Branch (202) 343-9226 Brennan.ross@epa.gov
Development of a sun safety fact sheet for individuals with darker skin	A fact sheet providing sun safety information for individuals with darker skin types will be developed.	Individuals with darker skin, who may mistakenly think they are not at risk, will have access to an easy-to-understand fact sheet that describes pertinent information on skin cancer, cataracts and the other health effects from UV radiation.	NA	Reduced exposure to UV radiation	Ross Brennan, Chief Stratospheric Program Implementation Branch (202) 343-9226 Brennan.ross@epa.gov

Activities	Output	Outcome			Point of Contact
		Short-term	Intermediate	Long-term	
Proposed rule on N-Propyl Bromide	The proposed rule will protect users of spray adhesives containing N-propyl bromide, a substitute for ozone-depleting substances. EPA is currently seeking comment on two proposed approaches to addressing exposure to n-propyl bromide by either 1) banning use of n-propyl bromide and requiring an alternative adhesive or 2) requiring users to reduce exposure to acceptable levels of n-propyl bromide and to monitor exposure of workers. Spray adhesives containing N-propyl bromide are used by several industries. Most workers in these industries are low-wage hourly workers, many of whom are Hispanic and female.	NA	NA	The proposed N-Propyl Bromide rule will affect approximately 12,000 people, reducing their exposure to this harmful solvent. Many of the affected industry workers are Hispanic and female.	Jeff Cohen, Chief Alternatives and Emissions Reduction Branch (202) 343-9005 Cohen.jeff@epa.gov

33

Office of Atmospheric Programs
(CY2007-FY2008)

Goal 1: Clean Air and Global Climate Change
Objective 1.5: Reduce Greenhouse Gas Emissions

Activities	Output	Outcome			Point of Contact
		Short-term	Intermediate	Long-term	
Climate Friendly Parks	Hawaiian native islanders will attend and participate in the Hawaii Volcanoes Workshop to learn about how climate change will/is affecting them.	This conference will increase Hawaiian Native Islander's understanding of climate change and its effects on indigenous communities in Hawaii.	NA	NA	Rona Birnbaum, Chief Climate Science and Impacts Branch (202) 343-9076 birnbaum.rona@epa.gov
Translation of documents related to international capacity building	Translation of documents into other languages. The ICBB will be translating several documents into Chinese and Spanish.	NA	NA	Providing documents in several languages will broaden access to climate change information and ensure that more people understand the issue of climate change.	Susan Wickwire, Chief International Capacity Building Branch (202) 343-9155 wickwire.susan@epa.gov
Translation of documents related to non-CO$_2$ programs	The Non-CO$_2$ Programs Branch (NCPB) will be translating several documents into Chinese and Spanish.	NA	NA	Providing documents in several languages will broaden access to non-CO$_2$ programs information and ensure that more people understand the issue of climate change.	Paul Gunning, Chief Non-CO$_2$ Programs Branch (202) 343-9736 Gunning.paul@epa.gov

34

Activities	Output	Outcome			Point of Contact
		Short-term	Intermediate	Long-term	
Sea Level Rise	Current activities include mapping elevations in the mid-Atlantic and mapping areas where shores will be protected as the sea level rises along the Atlantic and Gulf Coasts.	NA	NA	Mapping information will be useful to, and by, potentially vulnerable coastal communities.	Rona Birnbaum, Chief Climate Science and Impacts Branch (202) 343-9076 birnbaum.rona@epa.gov

35

Office of Atmospheric Programs
(CY2007-FY2008)

Goal 1: Clean Air and Global Climate Change
Objective 1.6   Enhance Science and Research

Activities	Output	Outcome			Point of Contact
		Short-term	Intermediate	Long-term	
Increase tribes' air quality monitoring capabilities	The Clean Air Status and Trends Network (CASTNET) program is working with Region VII to temporarily loan a sulfur dioxide and carbon monoxide gas analyzer to the Winnebego Tribe in Nebraska.	CASTNET will provide two trace-level gas analyzers (SO_2 and CO) and associated equipment to EPA Region VII who will be working with the Winnebego Tribe to operate them.	The region is helping the tribe set up a monitoring site and will be training tribal personnel to support the operation, calibration, and auditing of the trace-gas analyzers, among other measurements. The analyzers are hourly measurement systems which are consistent with the National Core Network (NCORE) approved methods and will benefit the Region and State if the tribal organization gains experience with this type of monitoring equipment.	Enhanced ability of tribes to develop and run their environmental programs which help to protect their communities and environment. Shared access to regional data used to monitor long-term trends in air pollution and to understand the behavior of atmospheric pollutants.	Rick Haeuber, Chief Assessment and Communications Branch (202) 343-9250 Haeuber.richard@epa.gov

36

Goal 1: Clean Air and Global Climate Change
Objective 1.1   Healthier Outdoor Air, Ozone and $PM_{2.5}$ (e.g., reduce asthma triggers such as particulate matter)

Activities	Output	Applicable Outcome Measure			Point of Contact
		Short-term (awareness)	Intermediate (behavior)	Long-term (condition)	
The National Clean Diesel Campaign (NCDC) and Clean School Bus USA will reduce diesel particulate matter and other air toxics from diesel engine exhaust by: 1. reducing all unnecessary idling from diesel engines by 2014 2. retrofitting, replacing or upgrading all 11 million existing mobile source engines by 2014.	Direct funding to 90% of NCDC projects and 100% of Clean School Bus USA projects to susceptible populations Direct 50% of all project funding to high asthma areas Direct 20% of the school bus funding to projects in urban, low-income areas. Direct 30% of the NCDC funded projects to areas with disproportionate amount of diesel pollution.	Make informational materials and web site available to communities nationwide.	Reduce unnecessary idling by all school bus drivers nationwide. School districts will adopt district-wide idling reduction policies. School districts will implement idling reduction campaign in their district. # drivers trained, # buses in fleet. Retrofit/replace 11 million engines nationwide.	Reduce public health risks (cancer and other non-cancer health effects) for people nationwide from exposure to the pollutants in diesel exhaust.	Steve Albrink Office of Transportation and Air Quality Tel : 202-343-9671 Email : albrink.steve@epa.gov

Goal 1: Clean Air and Global Climate Change
Objective 2: Reduce exposure to air toxics

Activities	Output	Applicable Outcome Measure			Point of Contact
		Short-term (awareness)	Intermediate (behavior)	Long-term (condition)	
Improve tools and guidance for predicting localized toxics impacts of transportation projects.	Develop enhanced HAPEM exposure model to better account for near-roadway environments. Issue draft guidance on predicting concentrations of toxic pollutants in the vicinity of proposed transportation projects.	National, state, and local assessments can include the effects of existing and proposed transportation projects.	Federal, state, and local governments can implement mitigation or other risk reduction measures during transportation planning. Communities can select appropriate local risk reduction measures.	Reduce risk of cancer and other non-cancer health effects for people living, working, and recreating near major roads.	Kathryn Sargeant Office of Transportation and Air Quality Tel : 734-214-4441 Email : sargeant.kathryn@epa.gov

38

Office of Transportation and Air Quality
(CY2007-CY2008)

Goal 1: Clean Air and Global Climate Change
Objective 1.1   Healthier Outdoor Air, Ozone and PM$_{2.5}$ (e.g., reduce asthma triggers such as particulate matter)

Activities	Output	Applicable Outcome Measure			Point of Contact
		Short-term (awareness)	**Intermediate** (behavior)	**Long-term** (condition)	
EPA's SmartWay Transport Partnership's (SWT) Innovative Financing Program. SWT is a collaborative program that creates market-based incentives that challenge the freight industry to improve its environmental performance while reducing operating cost and providing greater energy security. SWT's Financing Program goal is to develop sustainable financing strategies to provide truck companies and owner-operators access to financing options to help pay for technologies that not only reduce fuel use and air pollution but also subsequent impacts to communities.	SWT's mainstay is the SmartWay Upgrade Kit and "SmartWay Truck." SWT Upgrade Kits and Truck involve making a truck cleaner and energy efficient. The Kit consists of idle reduction, aerodynamics, and emissions control technologies. To encourage adoption of these devices, SWT creates low cost financial incentives. Upgrade trucks financed with SWT's low interest program are less expensive than the same truck not upgraded. SWT also seeks to reduce emissions from drayage and regional trucks which are frequently older, emit more air pollutants, and often have low-income and minority drivers.	SWT, with the Small Business Administration US Department of Agriculture (USDA) and others creates, educates, and markets various low cost financial opportunities to the trucking industry and owners. The USDA program involves working with community development banks to assist trucking companies located in rural areas which may also include low income or minority areas.	SWT encourages key changes in freight transport that leads to the adoption of clean, more efficient technologies: - Availability of lower cost loans through community development banks - Presence of truck dealerships and service centers capable and willing to install SmartWay Upgrade Kits - Participation of areas designated by EPA as nonattainment or maintenance for ozone and/or particulate matter.	Combined, SWT upgrades achieve reductions of up to 19% in oxides of nitrogen (NOx) and a 50-80% in particulate matter (PM). Overall, SWT reduces fuel use, operating costs, and emissions including air toxics associated with freight transportation. Specifically, by 2012, SWT aims to save 150 million barrels of oil (equal to 12 million cars off the road), reduce 200,000 tons of NOx plus PM and air toxics, and eliminate 33-66 million metric tons of CO2 per year.	Victor McMahan SmartWay Transport Partnership 202-343-9363 mcmahan.victor@epa.gov

39

Goal 4: Healthy Communities and Ecosystems
Objective 2: Collaborative problem-solving to address environmental justice issues

Activities	Output	Applicable Outcome Measure			Point of Contact
		Short-term (awareness)	Intermediate (behavior)	Long-term (condition)	
Phase II of the Baltimore Region Environmental Justice and Transportation Project (BREJTP) in cooperation with Morgan State University. Having completed Phase I of the project, "Community Outreach," involving a regional community-level needs assessment and review of technical methods to support environmental justice (EJ) analysis; Phase II, "Integration of Analytical Tools," will respond to community needs identified in Phase I - with follow-up analysis - and develop EJ Transportation Toolkit (EJTK) to fully incorporate EJ analysis into regional planning.	Phase II to develop and apply EJTK through case studies of air quality and accessibility issues in representative EJ communities. The methodology to involve series of steps to engage the cooperation of community stakeholders and various agencies. Steps include: a.) Problem definition (how widespread), b.) Framing impacts (critical variables), c.) Selection/Application of analytical techniques (spatial level), and d.) Resolution/Feedback (evaluation of the tools).	Measurable air quality and transport awareness and improvements in the region. Region has one of the nation's worst ozone problems affecting approx. 2.4 million people, ozone levels exceeded Federal standards nearly every summer for past 20 years under the former 1-hour standard, designated as "nonattainment" for PM2.5 and a significant asthma problem with the greatest impact to children.	EJ-related air quality and transportation issues are better identified and addressed by all relevant agencies in the region using the enhanced community involvement and technical analysis procedures in the EJTK, which in turn is fully integrated into regional transportation planning by 2008	Improved ability of relevant agencies to access environmental impacts, reduce mobile source criteria pollutants and air toxics and improve community benefits via transport facilities and services in EJ communities and Greater Baltimore region by 2008. EJTK replicated in other regions as community-based planning tool to assist users to identify and address challenges, requirements, and potential solutions to EJ-related transport issues.	Victor McMahan OTAQ, (202) 343-9363, mcmahan.victor@epa.gov

40

Community Action for a Renewed Environment (CARE) Program
(CY2007-FY2008)

Goal 4: Healthy Communities and Ecosystems
Objective 2: Collaborative problem-solving to address environmental justice issues

Activities	Output	Applicable Outcome Measure			Point of Contact
		Short-term (awareness)	Intermediate (behavior)	Long-term (condition)	
CARE Annual Training Workshop	Continue supporting the annual CARE Training Workshop for grantees and EPA staff.	Educate community partnerships about EPA resources and tools.	Increase awareness of implementation techniques and tools to reduce toxic risks.	Contribute to the reduction of toxic risks in the community.	Marva King CARE Program Coordinator (202) 564-2599 King.marva@epa.gov
		Increase trust among the Training Workshop participants.	Strengthen relationships between grantees and EPA staff.	Contribute to future partnership endeavors between communities and EPA.	Larry Weinstock CARE Grants Team Lead (202) 564-9226 Weinstock.larry@epa.gov
CARE Training Team	Establish monthly topic training sessions for the CARE projects.	Educate communities on topics of interest to them (i.e., pollution prevention, healthy homes, etc.)	Increase awareness of implementation techniques and tools to reduce toxic risks.	Contribute to the reduction of toxic risks in the community.	Marva King CARE Program Coordinator (202) 564-2599 King.marva@epa.gov
	Establish training for new regional CARE Project Officers.	Educate Regional CARE Project Officers to working in a community driven program where projects are in EJ areas.	Strengthen regional CARE staff expertise. Ensure regional staff becomes more familiar with EJ and CARE connection.	Contribute to overall sustainability of CARE program at the regional level.	Larry Weinstock CARE Grants Team Lead (202) 564-9226 Weinstock.larry@epa.gov
CARE Grants Team	Conduct National Question and Answer CARE Webcast Internet and Conference Calls for potential applicants.	Communicate the opportunity of the CARE program	Increase the knowledge of potential applicants including those in EJ communities.	Increase the overall numbers of applications received.	Larry Weinstock CARE Grants Team Lead (202) 564-9226 Weinstock.larry@epa.gov Marva King CARE Program Coordinator (202) 564-2599 King.marva@epa.gov

Activities	Output	Applicable Outcome Measure			Point of Contact
		Short-term (awareness)	Intermediate (behavior)	Long-term (condition)	
CARE Outreach and Communication	Create various marketing avenues for the program.	Produce quarterly CARE highlights, present CARE successes at conferences, and exhibit CARE.	Increase the awareness of the CARE community successes.	Assist in the overall knowledge of and the sustainability for the CARE program.	Larry Weinstock CARE Grants Team Lead (202) 564-9226 Weinstock.larry@epa.gov Marva King CARE Program Coordinator (202) 564-2599 King.marva@epa.gov
CARE External Liaison Team	Establish collaborative partnerships with various non-EPA entities.	Increase willingness of broader partnerships to assist CARE communities	Structure CDC and EPA collaboration, sustain ABA support, and increase APHA and NACCHO support.	Assist in the overall knowledge of and the sustainability for the CARE program.	Larry Weinstock CARE Grants Team Lead (202) 564-9226 Weinstock.larry@epa.gov Marva King CARE Program Coordinator (202) 564-2599 King.marva@epa.gov
CARE Administrative Team	NAPA evaluation of the CARE program.	Continue to provide support to NAPA evaluating the overall program.	Increase awareness of lessons learned and best practices in the CARE program.	Assist in the overall knowledge of and the sustainability for the CARE program.	Larry Weinstock CARE Grants Team Lead (202) 564-9226 Weinstock.larry@epa.gov Marva King CARE Program Coordinator (202) 564-2599 King.marva@epa.gov